PRENTICE HALL FOUNDATIO

MW00340397

Virgil Aldrich	Philosophy of Art
William Alston	Philosophy of Language
David Braybrooke	Philosophy of Social Science
Roderick M. Chisholm	Theory of Knowledge, 3E
William Dray	Philosophy of History
C. Dyke	Philosophy of Economics
Joel Feinberg	Social Philosophy
Frederick Ferré	Philosophy of Technology
William K. Frankena	Ethics, 2E
Martin P. Golding	Philosophy of Law
Carl Hempel	Philosophy of Natural Science
John Hick	Philosophy of Religion, 3E
David L. Hull	Philosophy of Biological Science
Gerald C. MacCallum	Political Philosophy
D.L. C. Maclachlan	Philosophy of Perception
Joseph Margolis	Philosophy of Psychology
Wesley C. Salmon	Logic, 3E
Jerome Shaffer	Philosophy of Mind
Richard Taylor	Metaphysics, 3E

Elizabeth Beardsley and Tom L. Beauchamp, Editors
Monroe Beardsley, Founding Editor

PHILOSOPHY OF PERCEPTION

D. L. C. Maclachlan
Queen's University at Kingston

PRENTICE HALL, *Englewood Cliffs, New Jersey 07632*

Library of Congress Cataloging-in-Publication Data

Maclachlan, D. L. C.
  Philosophy of perception.

  (Prentice-Hall foundations of philosophy series)
  Includes index.
  1. Perception (Philosophy) I. Title. II. Series.
B828.45.M33   1989   121'.3   88-4172
ISBN   0-13-662271-2

Editorial/production supervision: Linda B. Pawelchak
Manufacturing buyer: Peter Havens

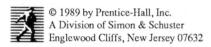 © 1989 by Prentice-Hall, Inc.
A Division of Simon & Schuster
Englewood Cliffs, New Jersey 07632

Printed in the United States of America
10 9 8 7 6 5 4 3 2

ISBN   0-13-662271-2

Prentice-Hall International (UK) Limited, *London*
Prentice-Hall of Australia Pty. Limited, *Sydney*
Prentice-Hall Canada Inc., *Toronto*
Prentice-Hall Hispanoamericana, S. A, *Mexico*
Prentice-Hall of India Private Limited, *New Delhi*
Prentice-Hall of Japan, Inc., *Tokyo*
Simon & Schuster Asia Pte. Ltd., *Singapore*
Editora Prentice-Hall do Brasil, Ltda., *Rio de Janeiro*

for my wife
Janet Faddies

Contents

Index   123

Foundations of Philosophy

Many of the problems of philosophy are of such broad relevance to human concerns, and so complex in their ramifications, that they are, in one form or another, perennially present. Though in the course of time they yield in part to philosophical inquiry, they may need to be rethought by each age in the light of its broader scientific knowledge and deepened ethical and religious experience. Better solutions are found by more refined and rigorous methods. Thus, one who approaches the study of philosophy in the hope of understanding the best of what it affords will look for both fundamental issues and contemporary achievements.

Written by a group of distinguished philosophers, the Foundations of Philosophy Series aims to exhibit some of the main problems in the various fields of philosophy as they stand at the present stage of philosophical history.

While certain fields are likely to be represented in most introductory courses in philosophy, college classes differ widely in emphasis, in method of instruction, and in rate of progress. Every instructor needs freedom to change his course as his own philosophical interests, the size and makeup of his class, and the needs of his students vary from year to year. The volumes in the Foundations of Philosophy Series—each complete in itself, but complementing the others—offer a new flexibility to the instructor, who can create his own textbook by combining several volumes as he wishes, and choose different combinations at different times. Those volumes that are not used in an introductory course will be found valuable, along with other texts or collections of readings, for the most specialized upper-level courses.

Elizabeth Beardsley / *Monroe Beardsley* / *Tom L. Beauchamp*

Preface

This book is designed as an introduction to the problem of perception through the exposition and defense of what may be regarded as the traditional theory. It is not, however, a historical account of the development of that theory, which since the rise of modern science—because of the rise of modern science—has dominated philosophical thought. Certain historical figures, such as Descartes, Locke, and Berkeley, do, indeed, appear from time to time in the following pages; but the main thrust of the book is the systematic deployment of the argument which supports the traditional theory.

The essence of this theory is that our knowledge of the world around us depends upon certain effects which are produced in us by the things in our environment—those effects being immediately accessible in experience in a way in which the external causes are not. This theory has had an immense appeal for various reasons, including its plausible explanation of perceptual errors in a way which is consonant with what is known about the physical and physiological conditions of perception. In recent years, it has lost its appeal for professional philosophers, although it still retains its grip in the wider intellectual community. I hope to show, however, by a careful development of the argument, that the difficulties usually associated with the traditional theory can be largely overcome.

Because the main function of the book is to introduce the problem of perception to students with no prior knowledge of the subject, the foundation laid in earlier chapters is perhaps more elaborate than would be otherwise necessary. Therefore, the chapters likely to be of greatest interest to those who are already familiar with this topic are Chapter Seven, in which the alternative "Theory of Appearing" is discussed, and Chapters Ten through Fourteen, in which an attempt is made to handle the standard objections.

The doctrine explained in the following pages is, I believe, the truth, although not necessarily the whole truth. It is the truth to the extent that the truth can be presented within the limits of a certain idiom or conceptual system. There may be more to be said, once the limits of this system of ideas have been transcended. But any theory employing a richer set of concepts must be able to incorporate the element of truth contained in the traditional explanation, so that a sound grasp of the traditional theory is at least a necessary first step in the dialectical development of a doctrine which goes beyond the standard causal representative theory. For this reason, I believe that the best possible introduction to the problem of perception is the presentation of a version of the traditional theory which is not aborted prematurely by an unwarranted collapse in the face of inconclusive evidence.

The argument of the book can be divided into two parts, with Chapters One to Nine presenting *The Road to Solipsism,* and Chapters Ten to Fourteen explaining *The Way Back. I*n the nature of the case, the second part *The Way Bac*k is more difficult than the first part. Although the first part contains some original arguments and observations, basically the road to solipsism is well trodden and familiar. It is the way back that is tricky.

I wish to thank Jackie Doherty, Linda Hall, Karen Hermer, and Ann Liblik for their invaluable assistance in the preparation of the manuscript.

CHAPTER ONE

Perception and Empirical Knowledge

The members of the human race possess a vast store of knowledge and information about the world in which they live—a knowledge that guides them in their conduct of practical affairs. Certainly, there are also error and ignorance, but even those who are comparatively ignorant and ill-informed possess an astonishing amount of correct information. There is no need to be surprised that we do not know everything: the wonder is that we know as much as we do.

This knowledge of the world is commonly called *empirical* knowledge and is contrasted with other types of knowledge, such as the *a priori* knowledge available in logic and mathematics or the knowledge of right and wrong, if the latter is indeed admitted as a kind of knowledge. Empirical knowledge is knowledge of the things and persons that exist in the actual world—knowledge of their natures, properties, and relationships. We have *a priori* mathematical knowledge that two plus two equals four but empirical knowledge that the number of columns in the Lincoln Memorial equals thirty-six. We have moral knowledge that it is wrong to bring about the deaths of innocent people but empirical knowledge that Hitler brought about the deaths of millions.

HOW DO WE KNOW WHAT WE KNOW?

Whenever someone claims to know a certain empirical fact, there is one question which it is always possible to ask: "How do you know?" ("How did you come to know?") This is always a possible question, even if it would sometimes be an odd one to ask in ordinary contexts. If Jim reports that the cat is on the mat, and I can see Jim gazing in the general direction of the mat, it would be very odd for me to ask "How do you know?" But it would be odd not because I am asking an illegitimate question without a proper answer but because I must already know the obvious answer to my question. Jim knows that the cat is on the mat because he can see it in front of his eyes. Although the question "How do you know?" may be idle and unnecessary in ordinary life, it is always legitimate in the sense that there always is, or should be, an appropriate answer available.

The philosopher who is interested in the problem of knowledge asks this simple "How do you know?" question in a completely general way. How do we know the great variety of things which we normally claim to know? When the question is put in this way, it may evoke a very small twinge of fear in some readers. If it does, this is because it has introduced the "Bogey of Scepticism," the suspicion that our claims to knowledge are not securely founded. The question "How do you know?" is often asked in particular cases in ordinary life because the speaker has his or her doubts about the claim to knowledge that is being made. These doubts are reinforced if no satisfactory answer is forthcoming. Dismayed by the scope of the philosopher's version of the question, we may be afraid that no adequate answer can be provided. Throughout the history of philosophy, this worry about scepticism has been a perennial concern. Once the worm of doubt is introduced, we have a powerful motive for investigating the topic of knowledge. Not that this is the only reason for an interest in the subject. Even if you do not share the fear that the whole edifice of our knowledge may turn out to be built upon sand, you may have enough healthy curiosity to ask at some point in your life how we do find out the things which we claim to know about the world in which we live.

This is a very general question which can be given only a very general answer. There is no prospect of explaining in detail how each piece of empirical knowledge has been acquired. All we can hope for is an account of the general ways in which we gain knowledge of the world. Provided that we do not dig too deeply, such an account can be given quickly and easily. This is the simple task that will occupy the remainder of this chapter. No great surprises are to be expected. The analysis given will be very straightforward and commonsensical. You may even get the feeling that you have learned nothing new. Nevertheless, the explicit statement and methodical arrangement of a number of obvious truths is an important first step in the investigation. It is well worthwhile to be reminded of what you already know, especially if you have never before formulated your knowledge in this abstract and general way.

SENSE PERCEPTION

One obvious way in which we get to know about our environment is through sense perception, through the use of the various senses with which we have been provided. If I am asked how I know that there is a table in front of my eyes, I answer: "Because I can see it." If I am asked how I know that a noisy car is passing outside, I answer: "Because I can hear it." If I am asked how I know that there is a dead rat under the floorboards, I answer: "Because I can smell it." Traditionally, there are five main senses— the sense of sight, the sense of hearing, the sense of touch, the sense of taste, and the sense of smell. Others can be added to the list, such as the sense of temperature, the sense of pain, and what is sometimes called the *kinesthetic* sense, which informs us about the movement and position of the various parts of our bodies. Through the judicious use of my senses, I can discover a great deal about the present nature of my immediate environment.

MEMORY

Although the faculty of sense perception may be invoked to explain my knowledge of what is now going on in my vicinity, the present range of my knowledge extends far beyond the present range of my senses. For one thing, I possess a great deal of knowledge about the past. To explain this, another faculty must be introduced —the faculty of memory. If I am asked how I know that Joan was here yesterday, I might very well say: "Because I saw her"; but this is not the complete explanation. For me to know that Joan was here yesterday, seeing her yesterday is not enough. It is also essential that I now remember having seen her yesterday. Thus, a full explanation of my knowledge of Joan's presence yesterday requires the introduction of the faculty of memory. Memory is not, of course, in itself a way of getting to know about the world: it is rather a way of retaining knowledge acquired in other ways. Nevertheless, memory is a necessary ingredient in any explanation of our knowledge of the past.

INFERENCE

Even when supplemented by the faculty of memory to retain the knowledge we acquire, the faculty of sense perception is not enough to account for all the knowledge we possess. It does not, for instance, explain our knowledge of the future. We do know things which will definitely happen and many more things which definitely will not. For example, astronomers are able to predict with absolute accuracy the date of the next eclipse of the moon; I now with equal certainty that I will not grow to a height of twelve feet during the next six months. But how do we know the date of the next lunar eclipse and that adults will not suddenly double their height? The answer is that we make *inferences* based on past experience. Ancient astronomers first learned to predict eclipses when they noticed regularities in the patterns of eclipses in the past. Assuming that this regularity would continue in the future, they were able to infer when the next eclipse would occur. I infer that I shall not suddenly double in height because I have never known that to happen to an adult human being. Inferences based on past experience are essential if we are to know anything about what will happen in the future, but they also yield important information about what has happened in the past and about what is happening now beyond the range of the senses. For example, the detective did not see the burglar climbing in through the window, but he infers that this must have happened when he finds the window forced open and the jewelry gone.

AUTHORITY

There is one important factor in our acquisition of information which I have so far ignored. The vast majority of our beliefs are not based on first-hand evidence at all, but on what we have learned from other people. We gather a great deal of information in conversation with other people, and more from books and newspapers, radio and television. Beliefs acquired in this way may be called "beliefs based on authority," although this is to stretch the use of the word *authority*, since there are many sources of information which we would not be prepared to dignify with the title of authorities in the usual sense. I would believe you if you told me that there was a sparrow in the garden without considering you an authority on birds.

It is true enough that our authorities are sometimes unreliable, particularly when the term is used in its extended sense. You can't believe everything you are told; you can't believe everything you read in the newspaper. Nevertheless, it is equally true that you cannot function in this life unless you accept, by and large, what you are told by other people. You have to be careful, but you can't check up on everything.

Although information based on the authority of others is of enormous practical importance, it is of little theoretical interest because it is not an original way of acquiring knowledge about the world. Even if I personally acquire a piece of information by relying on my authorities, what I find out in this way must have been discovered originally in some other way. My authority may herself have acquired the information from someone else, but ultimately there must be someone who has discovered it for himself through sense perception or inference, which are the two original sources of empirical knowledge. Memory, as already explained, is not strictly a source of knowledge, but a faculty through which we retain knowledge we have already acquired.

SENSE PERCEPTION AS FUNDAMENTAL SOURCE OF KNOWLEDGE

Of the two original sources of empirical knowledge, it is sense perception which appears to be fundamental. Empirical inferences always require a basis in sense perception. For example, the inference that a burglar has climbed in through the window depends on the perception that the window is open and damaged plus memories of past sense experiences that indicate how this kind of damage is likely to be produced. There is no similar basis required for my knowledge that there is a table in front of my eyes. I know that there is a table before me because I can see it. That is all there is to it, or so it seems.

Thus, the procedure to be adopted in explaining and justifying a given piece of empirical knowledge would appear to be this. We must trace the knowledge back to its original sources in sense experience. In practice, this is often extremely complicated. For example, I know the date of the next eclipse of the moon because I read it in *Old Moore's Almanac*. Old Moore, or the astronomer he consulted, has discovered the date by making the necessary calculations and inferences. These inferences in turn are based on observational data provided by the past sense experiences of a variety of observers. Direct observation by means of the senses is the foundation of empirical knowledge, however elaborate the superstructure we build on this foundation through techniques of empirical inference.

This simple answer to the original question about how we acquire empirical knowledge is obviously not the final solution to the problem. Indeed, so far I have done little more than establish a framework in terms of which other problems can be posed. There is a problem about sense perception, which I have taken to be the foundation of empirical knowledge. There is a problem about memory, through which we retain the knowledge acquired in the past. And there is a problem about the justification of the empirical inferences through which we reach conclusions which go beyond the data supplied by sense experience. This book will concentrate on the first of these great problems — the problem of perception. I shall say virtually nothing about the problem of memory, assuming in a simpleminded way that the faculty of memory is somehow capable of preserving past experience and knowledge. It will be necessary, however, to say more about the problem of empirical inference, which will turn out to be more intimately connected with the problem of perception than it might appear at first sight.

CHAPTER TWO

What Do We Really Hear?

In the first chapter, it was shown that sense perception has a peculiarly fundamental part to play in our knowledge of the things in the world. It is by sense perception, by using my eyes, that I know that there is at present a table in this room. When I leave the room, I will know that there *was* a table in the room because I will remember seeing it when I was in the room. Granted, an act of memory is involved, but my past sense experience is equally essential. Also, after leaving the room, I will be able to infer that the table is *still* in the room if I take up a position guarding the door and make sure that no one carries the table away. This inference depends not only on my perception of the table when I was in the room but also on my knowledge of the habits of tables and other similar objects — a knowledge built up as a result of past sense experiences. I know that the table is not the sort of thing that might be folded up and smuggled out in someone's pocket. Finally, someone else who is prepared to accept my authority as a reliable source of information may come to know what I know about the table if I convey my knowledge in a suitable way. The knowledge which I convey will be based either on my current sense experience, or on my memory of past experiences, or on an inference which I draw from data provided in sense experience. Thus, although it is possible to answer the question: "How do you know?" by saying "I was told," "I infer," or "I remember," as well as by saying "I perceive," all the other answers ultimately depend on knowledge acquired through sense perception.

In most circumstances, if I am asked how I know that there is a table in the room, the answer "Because I can see it" would be accepted as a satisfactory final answer and no further questions would be asked. Again, if I am asked how I know that there is a car passing the window, the answer "Because I can hear it" would also give the questioner complete satisfaction. In general, it seems that I can give a final answer to questions about how I know the presence of particular objects by saying that I perceive these objects. However, from a philosophical point of view, such answers cannot be accepted as final answers. It is necessary to dig more deeply. To show that the situation is not as straightforward as it may appear, let us begin with the sense of hearing.

WHAT DO WE HEAR BUT SOUNDS AND NOISES?

Suppose there is a car passing the window. I am asked how I know that there is a car passing the window and I answer: "Because I can hear it." Again, suppose that there is a burglar moving about downstairs. I am asked how I know that there is a burglar downstairs and I answer: "Because I can hear him." Usually we would be perfectly happy to accept these answers as quite satisfactory, unless, for example, we had reason to believe that the burglar downstairs was only the cat. But do we really hear the car passing the window and the burglar downstairs? Isn't what we actually hear no more than the noise made by the car passing the window and the noise made by the burglar moving about downstairs? In general, do we ever hear anything except sounds and noises of various kinds? Isn't it true that when a car passes the window, all we really hear is a certain sort of sound, and we say that we hear a car only because we assume that there is a car making the sound we hear? In the other case, all I really hear are certain suspicious noises, and I say I hear a burglar only because I assume that a burglar is responsible for the suspicious noises in question.

Therefore, a philosopher can no longer accept: "Because I can hear it" as a final answer to the question: "How do you know that there is a car passing the window?" The knowledge of the car passing is based on evidence which is nothing more than a certain sort of sound. From the sound, which is all that we really hear, it is necessary to infer the existence of the car that is responsible for the sound. We have had plenty of experience of cars and the noises they make. Hearing again a noise of the kind we associated with cars in the past, we infer that a car is responsible for the present noise.

USING INFERENCE

In the preliminary classification of the first chapter, I contrasted knowledge by perception and knowledge by inference. "Hearing a car passing" was classified as knowledge by perception. It now appears that this was a mistake. In the case of hearing, by direct perception we know only sounds and noises. The objects responsible for these sounds and noises must be inferred.

In arguing that the things which we say we hear are really inferred, I am not suggesting, of course, that we go through some explicit verbal performance of inferring. When I infer that there is a dog in the vicinity responsible for the barking noise I directly experience, I do not catch myself saying (either out loud or even under my breath): "I hear a barking noise. Barking noises are usually made by dogs. Therefore, there must be a dog in the neighborhood making *this* barking noise." Indeed, even the conclusion of this inference is often not expressed in language.

Inferring, however, is not a mental act which necessarily requires the use of language. Indeed, the expression of an inference in language is the exception and not the rule. In the last chapter, I introduced the detective who infers that the burglar must have climbed through the window when he finds the window forced open and the jewelry gone. Although the detective may set out his premises and conclusion in verbal form for the benefit of his new assistant, he may also perform the act of inference without using words at all. If he goes out to look for footprints in the soft earth in front of the window, he shows that he has drawn the appropriate conclusion, even if he has said nothing at all, not even under his breath.

It is easy to overlook the element of inference involved in the case of hearing, not only because the inference is usually nonverbal but also because the identification of the object responsible for the noise is often so swift and virtually automatic. But from time to time we come across unfamiliar noises which we cannot identify right away. Then the nature of the intellectual process, which is arrested in mid-course, becomes clear. If we cannot tell immediately what is making a certain noise, we have to try to remember when we heard a similar noise before and what was making it. If we are successful in this, we can infer what is probably responsible for the present noise. But whether the inference is swift and spontaneous or slow and deliberate, the movement of thought is essentially the same.

Inferences of a nonverbal and undramatic kind actually play a much wider role in the constitution of our knowledge than we normally recognize. For example, I believe that on a hill overlooking the city of Kingston, Ontario, there is a massive fortification called Fort Henry. I do not normally think of myself as inferring the existence of this structure, since I have seen it many times with my own eyes. But although I may claim that the fort was there yesterday because I remember seeing it yesterday, how do I know that it is still there today? Since I do not happen to be seeing it at the moment, my belief in its continued existence must depend on an inference. This inference is based on my past experience of the habits of buildings like Fort Henry. I know from past experience that objects as bulky and solid as Fort Henry cannot be removed without the expenditure of a great deal of effort, time, and money. Therefore, in all probability, Fort Henry is still where it was the last time I saw it.

To say that I *infer* the continued existence of Fort Henry is perhaps to use the word *inference* in a wider sense than is customary in ordinary language. It would be more normal to say that I assume, suppose, or take for granted that Fort Henry is still there. It is customary to keep the term *inference* for cases in which something more closely approximating detective work is involved. There is, however, a fundamental similarity between cases where the acquisition of the belief is easy and automatic and cases where thought and deliberation are required. I want to use the word *inference* in a wide and general sense to mark this similarity. That is why I say that we *infer* the presence of the dog responsible for the barking noises.

MISTAKEN INFERENCES

When I rely on my sense of hearing to determine the nature of the objects in the vicinity, it is undeniable that I make an occasional mistake. Once the presence of an element of inference is recognized, we can see that many of these mistakes are due to the unreliability of our inferences, not to some defect in our sense of hearing. For example, if I say: "I hear a burglar downstairs" when it is really only the cat, I have made a mistake, not because I have poor hearing, but because I have drawn the wrong conclusion from the noises I heard. Even at the best of times, the inferences that we make from the noises we hear to the things we take to be responsible are not foolproof. These inferences are based on what we have normally found in the past to be responsible for sounds of certain kinds, but it is always possible for the present case to be an exception to the general rule. If I hear a barking noise it is certainly reasonable for me to infer that the noise is being made by a dog, since dogs are indeed responsible for most of the barking that occurs. But I may be wrong. Many human beings are quite good at imitating the barking of a dog, and I may be fooled by a skillful mimic.

It is worth pointing out that there is one way that we reduce the risk of error introduced by the fact that quite different things may produce rather similar sounds. We are guided by our assessment of what is likely in the particular situation. For example, if I know that George is following me along the path, I assume that it is George who is responsible for the sound of the footsteps I hear behind me, and not some man-eating monster, even if I know that George and man-eating monsters make very similar sounds. (If I heard the same sounds alone at night in the jungle, I might not be so quick to rule out the man-eating monster possibility.) Nevertheless, whatever precautions we may take, the risk of error can never be entirely eliminated.

ELLIPTICAL IDIOMS IN ORDINARY LANGUAGE

If we really hear only sounds and noises and have to infer the things that we take to be responsible, is it wrong to say things like "I hear a dog" or "I hear a train"? After all, if we really hear only sounds and noises, then we do not really hear dogs and trains, and if we do not really hear dogs and trains, then those who say "I hear a dog" or "I hear a train" must be mistaken. It appears, then, that a whole category of ordinary statements has been convicted of systematic error. If we want to say only what is strictly true, we must say "I hear a sound made by a dog" and not "I hear a dog."

Not that any recommendations which philosophers might make along these lines are likely to have any practical effect. Most people often speak quite loosely, being prepared to sacrifice precision in order to save time. They use elliptical idioms, which leave things out, when it is obvious how the blanks are to be filled in. It may be suggested that "I hear a dog" is an elliptical statement, abbreviating the more elaborate declaration "I hear a sound made by a dog." Since what is implicitly understood in the abbreviated version is perfectly clear, there is no loss in accuracy for practical purposes. Since I cannot hear a dog without hearing some sound made by the dog, it is unduly pedantic to say that I am hearing a sound made by a dog unless I have something specific to say about the nature of the sound. If I want to say "I heard the loud creak of the door opening," I have to say just that; but if I want to say merely "I heard the sound of the door opening," I might as well say "I heard the door opening."

DIRECT AND INDIRECT PERCEPTION

This explanation certainly justifies our current linguistic practices and shows that it is permissible and even advantageous to continue saying things like "I hear a dog" or "I hear the door." But it doesn't alter the fact that in all strictness we hear neither dogs nor doors but only certain sounds. In order to soften this conclusion, some philosophers have drawn a distinction between what we perceive directly and what we perceive indirectly. By the sense of hearing, we *directly* perceive, indeed, only certain sounds and noises, but we may say that we perceive *indirectly* the things responsible for these sounds and noises. What is directly perceived is what is actually given in sense experience, but we may legitimately say that we perceive (indirectly) many things which we merely *infer* from what is actually given. We do not, of course, perceive indirectly everything which is inferred from what is directly perceived. I may very well infer the lack of oil in the engine from the loud thumping noise I hear, but I do not want to say that I hear the lack of oil in the engine, even indirectly. The point of introducing a distinction between direct and indirect perception is not to extend the range of things which we may say that we hear, see, taste, or perceive through the other senses: the purpose is to subdivide into two classes the things that we already say we perceive in ordinary language. For example, the grammatical object following the verb "to hear" has two distinct functions: it may be used to indicate the sound or noise which is heard; or it may be used to indicate the source of the sound or noise. The heard sounds may be classed as *direct objects of perception* and the inferred sources as *indirect objects of perception.*

The main conclusion of this chapter, that we must infer the sources of the sounds we hear, can hardly be said to be particularly novel and exciting. Even if you have never thought about auditory experience in this abstract and general way, the conclusion which I have reached may seem to you more a matter of making explicit what you have always known implicitly, rather than the revelation of a completely new truth. The importance of this account of hearing, however, is that it provides us with a model which may be applied in other areas with more exciting results. It supplies us with a set of ideas or conceptual scheme in terms of which we may attempt to interpret other parts of our experience. The analysis of the sense of hearing shows that only sounds are directly perceived and that other things are inferred. We may also ask what is directly perceived and what is inferred in the case of each of the other senses.

INFERENCE AND THE SENSE OF SMELL

The sense of smell can be analyzed very easily and naturally along the same lines as the sense of hearing. Just as we sometimes say that we hear *things* (e.g., "I hear a dog") and sometimes say that we hear *sounds* (e.g., "I hear a barking noise"), so we sometimes say that we smell *things* (e.g., "I smell a rose"; "I smell the blood of an Englishman") and sometimes say that we smell *scents, odors,* and *smells* (e.g., "I smell the scent of a rose"; "I smell a peculiar odor"). Just as the barking noise is the direct object of perception from which we have to infer the dog responsible for the barking noise, so the smell is the direct object of perception from which we have to infer the thing that is responsible, based on our past experience of what has caused similar smells. When I say that I smell a dead rat under the floorboards, what I really smell is only a certain unpleasant odor. I infer that the smell is coming from a dead rat because I know from past experience that this is the sort of smell given off by dead rats. Such inferences depend not merely on the nature of the smell but also on general knowledge of what is likely in the situation. Even if I am quite unable to distinguish between the smell of a dead rat and the smell of a dead duck-billed platypus, I rule out the platypus since I know that such animals are to be found only in Australia. As we discovered in the case of hearing, the inferences which are made are never foolproof. I think that I smell a rat, but I may be wrong — the smell may be coming from a dead squirrel. Thus, only the smell is directly perceived; the rat must be inferred.

CHAPTER THREE

What Do
We Really See?

For human beings, the sense of sight is the most important source of detailed knowledge about the world. For other animals, other senses are more important. Some dogs have a very highly developed sense of smell, and the bat relies on its acute sense of hearing. But in the case of humans there is no doubt that the sense of sight has the dominant role. When we come to apply to the sense of sight the model developed in connection with hearing, we discover that the situation is a good deal more complicated than it was when the model was applied to the sense of smell. The sense of sight deserves a chapter to itself.

In Chapter Two, it was argued that we do not really hear all the things that we normally say we hear. We really hear only sounds and noises and must infer the things that we take to be responsible for these sounds and noises. Do we really see all the things that we normally say we see? And if not, what do we really see and what must we infer? To pose the same problem in terms of the notions of direct and indirect perception, what do we directly perceive through the sense of sight, and what is perceived only indirectly?

PRELIMINARY CASES

I shall begin with certain interesting cases in which it is perfectly clear that we really do not see things that it is natural to say we see. Suppose that the bus that I am expecting comes along a dusty road, throwing up such a cloud of dust that the bus itself is completely hidden. It would be quite natural for me to say that I see the bus coming, although it is obvious that I really see only the cloud of dust. Again, it is natural enough to say that I see a man who is in fact hiding behind a curtain if the curtain bulges in a way that betrays his presence. Nevertheless, I do not really see the man, but only the bulge in the curtain. The man behind the curtain must be inferred from the visible bulge. A third example was given by the seventeenth-century French philosopher Descartes in his "Meditations on the First Philosophy." Descartes takes the case of "human beings passing on in the street below, as observed from a window." He points out that although "I do not fail to say that I see the men themselves . . .yet what do I see from the window beyond hats and cloaks that might cover artificial machines, whose motions might be determined by springs?" (*A Discourse on Method, etc.,* trans. John Veitch, *Everyman's Library,* No. 570 [London: J.M. Dent & Sons Ltd., 1912], p. 92). Descartes ascribes the belief that there are human beings under the hats and cloaks to the faculty of judgment, but this differs only in terminology from my view that the human beings must be inferred.

These three cases clearly show that in everyday life we are indeed prepared to go beyond the actual visual evidence and claim that we see things that we really infer. I am now ready to move to the next sort of case in which we say that we see an object, even although only part of it is visible. Suppose that I am out working in my garden, and my neighbor Joan Smith is working in her garden next door. From where I am standing, I can see her head bobbing about on the other side of the hedge. Although it would be perfectly natural for me to say that I see Joan out in her garden, there is a sense in which all I see is Joan's head and not the complete Joan: the rest of her body is obscured by the hedge. That is, I have to *infer* that the complete Joan is out working in her garden on the other side of the hedge. I am quite prepared to make such an inference, because I know from past experience that a person's body usually accompanies his or her head wherever it goes. In this kind of case, indeed, I cannot deny that I really see Joan in the way in which I can deny that I really see a bus completely hidden by a cloud of dust. Just as hitting a part of a target is hitting the target, so seeing a part of an object is seeing the object, provided, of course, that the part seen has not become detached from the whole. Therefore, it would be wrong to say that I didn't see Joan but only her head, since this would suggest that the rest of Joan wasn't there. This does not alter the fact, however, that I do not see the *complete* person and that I must infer the rest of her from the parts visible above the hedge, which are alone directly perceived.

PERCEPTION OF SURFACES

But is it strictly true that I directly perceive even those parts of an object that are in full view? Do I directly perceive even Joan's head on the other side of the hedge? On reflection, it is clear that all I actually see when I look at a physical object is a part of its surface—that part of its surface which happens to be facing me at the time. If I am looking at a large wooden cube, I can see at best three of its six sides. No matter how I maneuver, I cannot see all six sides at once (unless I use mirrors). Nor can I see the inside of the cube, unless I break it up into pieces, and even then I cannot see inside the pieces. Thus, when I look at a physical object, what I actually see is not identical with the physical object that I believe to exist in front of me. The nature of the physical object and its unseen surfaces must be inferred from the surfaces which are seen. The table that I say I see is actually inferred from those parts of its surface that are visible from where I stand. I can make this inference because I know from past experience that the particular surface which I am seeing is characteristic of the kind of physical object I have been taught to call a table. In this case, it is extremely unlikely that the inference I am making is mistaken, but it is not impossible. It is just possible that the surface I am now seeing is not the surface of a table at all but the surface of a dummy table, made of thin paper stretched out over a wire frame and painted to look like solid wood. I have never actually seen a dummy table of the kind I have been describing, but I have seen and been fooled by fake chocolate which was really a piece of wood painted brown. Since the surface I saw was like the surface of real chocolate, I inferred that what I was seeing was real chocolate, and

I discovered my mistake only when I tried to eat it. The possibility of making mistakes like this confirms the view that I am actually inferring the physical things that I say I see. I made a mistake about the chocolate because I made an inference that was very reasonable in the circumstances but led to a false conclusion.

Thus, the things that we say we see in everyday life are many and various. Sometimes we say that we see part of the surface of a physical object; sometimes we say that we see part of the physical object; and sometimes we just say that we see the physical object. Sometimes, we even say that we see an object that is completely concealed from view if it betrays its presence in a particularly obvious way (e.g., by a bulge in a curtain). Of these various things that we say we see, only surfaces of physical objects are directly perceived, in the sense that they are perceived without being inferred from anything else. Physical objects and their parts are perceived only indirectly, and their presence must be inferred from the particular surfaces that are directly perceived. Although the perception of surfaces has this fundamental role in visual experience, it is in fact only rarely that we actually talk about seeing some particular surface because we are mainly interested in what sorts of things are around in the vicinity and not in the exact nature of the evidence presented in visual experience. A hunter in the jungle will say: "I see a tiger" because he is more interested in the presence of the tiger than in the nature of his visual experience. The hunter will not appreciate the precision of a philosopher who points out that he is really seeing only the front surface of a tiger.

Thus, it appears that the surfaces of physical objects are the direct objects of visual perception, just as sounds and noises are the direct objects of auditory perception. A little reflection, however, will show that in the case of vision, the situation is not as tidy as it is in the case of hearing. Surfaces are the direct objects of visual perception only when we are dealing with certain types of physical things. Suppose that instead of concentrating on opaque physical objects like tigers and tables, we were to take such things as transparent glass ashtrays, clear soup, mist and fog, shadows, flashes of light, and rainbows. All such things are certainly visible, but none of them are surfaces of physical objects, and none of them are inferred from the surfaces of physical objects. The items in this list of exceptions are both numerous and varied, and this may lead us to suspect that the doctrine that surfaces are direct objects of visual perception is not the last word on the subject, even in those cases in which, at first sight, it appears to be correct.

SIGHT AND HEARING COMPARED

When all the exceptions are taken into account, the result of our preliminary investigation of the sense of sight contrasts markedly with the simple, straightforward conclusion reached in the case of hearing where all the items directly perceived belong to the same category. Only sounds and noises are directly perceived, and everything else that we say we hear is inferred from certain sounds and noises. With sight, the surfaces of physical objects, if directly perceived at all, are not the only items directly perceived through the sense of sight. There are many items that we quite properly say we see, although we do not infer them from some surface of a physical object. It just so happens that there is no single sort of thing that we normally say we see and from which we infer all the other things that we say we see. Therefore, if we are to provide a unified theory of the direct object of visual perception, corresponding to the theory that sounds and only sounds are direct objects of auditory perception, it will be necessary to go beyond our ordinary ways of thinking and talking about visual experience. It will be necessary to find some item from which we infer surfaces of physical objects and shadows and flashes and everything else that we say we see. Since no such item can be identified at the level of commonsense, it must be introduced, if at all, by a philosophical argument.

The difference in the results we reached when dealing with sight and hearing is all the more surprising when we consider the close analogy between the physical processes through which the relevant sense organs are affected. When a dog barks, its vocal chords begin to vibrate. These vibrations cause a disturbance in the particles surrounding the vocal chords—a disturbance that is propagated as waves in all directions. When a segment of the wave-front reaches our ear, parts of the ear also begin to vibrate and then we hear the sound. A similar process occurs when we see a table. Light waves of various frequencies emitted by a source of light, such as the sun or a light bulb, fall upon the surface of the table. Some of these light waves are absorbed, and others are reflected. The physical character of the surface of the table determines which light waves are absorbed and which are reflected. A small sample of the light waves reflected by the table enters the eye, is focused by the lens in the eye, and is projected onto the sensitive area at the back of the eye called the retina. Then we see whatever it is that we do see.

There are certainly differences between the physical processes involved in seeing and hearing. There are differences in the structure of the sense organs employed, and there are also major differences between sound waves and the electromagnetic waves involved in visual perception. Nevertheless, the two sorts of processes exhibit a very striking fundamental similarity. The extent of the similarity is partly concealed by the particular examples I have chosen. When we hear a dog, the sound waves come to us in a direct line. When we see a table, the light waves involved are *reflected* light waves. This difference, however, is not an essential difference between hearing and seeing and is not always true. There are important exceptions. When we look at a star or at an electric light bulb, the light waves *are* coming in a direct line; and when we hear an echo, the sound waves have been reflected from some surface.

To make the analogy as close as possible, let us compare what happens when we see a table with what happens when we hear the echo produced by the reflection of the sound of the dog's barking from a conveniently placed cliff. In the one case, the eye is affected by light waves emitted by the sun or some other source of light, and reflected from the surface of the table; in the other case, the ear is affected by sound waves produced by the barking dog and reflected from the surface of the cliff. In spite of the strength of this analogy, the accounts of hearing and sight given so far would ascribe the objects directly perceived in the two cases to quite different categories. When we look at the table, we directly perceive the surface of the table; but in the other case, we directly perceive not the surface of the cliff, but an echo, which is a certain sort of sound. Indeed, it would be very odd to suggest that we heard the surface of the cliff at all. But why are we not allowed to say that we hear the surface of the cliff when we are permitted to say that we see the surface of the table? What justifies this distinction?

The probable explanation of the difference is that we can learn a great deal about surfaces from which light waves are reflected through our sense of sight, whereas what we can learn through our sense of hearing about the surfaces from which sound waves are reflected is almost negligible. We do, however, learn something from echos about the nature of our environment. For example, I can usually tell from the difference in the sounds I hear whether I am in a room or in the open air. We do not make much use of this vestigial power of echo location because we get so much better information from our sense of sight. But in the case of someone who is blind, this power is much more important and accounts for the uncanny success with which blind people avoid obstacles, although they have no sense of sight to provide the usual warnings.

Such a power of echo location is used even more extensively by bats. How can a creature such as a bat fly about at high speed in a pitch black room without collisions? The answer is that the bat emits a range of high pitched sounds and listens for the echos it gets when the sound waves are reflected by objects. From the character of the echos, the bat is able to determine the nature and position of the objects around it.

BATPEOPLE

It is by no means impossible that a race of intelligent beings might have developed who used their sense of hearing in much the same way as we use our sense of sight. Since there is nothing that is a constant source of sound waves in the way in which the sun is a constant source of light waves, such beings would have to be equipped, like the bat, with some means of making suitable sounds, such as whistles. Then, by listening to the echos, they would be able to determine the shape, size, and position of the surfaces from which the sound waves are reflected, just as we are able to determine the shape, size, and position of surfaces from which light waves are reflected by using our sense of sight. Such beings would not, indeed, be able to discriminate the color properties of surfaces, which are determined by the capacity of the surfaces to reflect or absorb light waves of specific wavelengths. They would, however, be able to detect acoustical properties of surfaces which are the counterparts of the color properties we detect by our sense of sight. The physical constitution of an object determines not only what light waves but also what sound waves are reflected from its surfaces. Just as different surfaces may have different color properties because of differing capacities to reflect light waves, so different surfaces may have different acoustical properties because of differing capacities to reflect sound waves. Walls covered with fabric have different acoustical properties from walls that are smoothly plastered.

A brief and appropriate way of referring to these intelligent beings I have introduced is to call them *batpeople*. Like the bat, they would have a power of hearing that matches our power of sight. They would be able to acquire just as detailed information about the size, shape, position, and acoustical properties of surfaces as we can acquire about the size, shape, position and color properties of surfaces. Thus, the batpeople would have just as good reasons for saying that they can hear the surfaces of physical things as we have for saying that we can see the surfaces of physical things.

Although we could hardly disallow the claim of the batpeople that they can hear the surfaces of physical things, we would never agree that it is these surfaces that are the direct objects of their sense of hearing. We would not withdraw our earlier conclusion that in the case of hearing, what we directly perceive are always sounds and nothing but sounds. The surfaces of physical things are indirect objects of auditory perception which the batpeople infer from the echos that are the direct objects. Given a certain sort of echo, the batpeople infer the character of the reflecting surface involved. They are licensed to say that they hear surfaces only in the way in which we are licensed to say that we hear dogs — when we infer the dogs from the sounds they are making.

SEEING LIGHT

I have invented this completely hypothetical race of batpeople because I believe that what we would say about their sense of hearing will throw light on what we should say, as philosophers, about our own sense of sight. If we insist that the batpeople really hear only the echos from which they infer the character of the perceived surfaces, must we not admit that we also infer the character of the surfaces which we say we see from something else that corresponds to the echos heard by the batpeople? But what could be this mysterious something else from which we infer the surfaces that we normally say we see? The counterpart in vision to sound in hearing is light. Must we say, then, that the direct object of visual perception is light or a pattern of light from which we infer the variously colored surfaces of physical things and all the other things that we say we see?

It is not, indeed, completely idiosyncratic to talk about seeing light. For instance, it seems quite natural to talk about seeing the light coming from a distant star. But to claim that in all cases of visual perception we really see only light is to revise quite drastically our ordinary ways of thinking about visual experience. In order to make the suggestion more intelligible and more acceptable, let us consider the matter from the point of view of the hypothetical batpeople, whom we shall now endow with a rudimentary visual sense. Let us suppose that they enjoy a vague visual experience when their rudimentary eyes are stimulated by a strong light. Although the batpeople are originally conscious of the physical objects in their environment through their sense of hearing, it would be possible for them to locate objects during periods of silence by relying on the visual evidence, just as we can locate objects in the dark through the sounds they make. In such cases, it is clear that we do not directly perceive the physical objects; instead, we infer the objects from the sounds we hear. Similarly, I suspect that the batpeople would think of objects located through their sense of sight as inferred from the visual evidence. If the batpeople were to hear of a race of beings like ourselves who relied on the sense of sight, they might indeed understand how natural it was for us to suppose that we directly perceived the surfaces of things through the sense of sight. Nevertheless, they would be quite convinced that we did not in fact have a direct visual perception of the surfaces of physical things. It is difficult to resist the conclusion that they would be right.

To sum up, the suggestion that through the sense of sight we directly perceive only patterns of light has two big points in its favor. In the first place, this suggestion gets rid of the untidiness of the original proposal according to which we directly perceive not only surfaces but also quite a variety of other items. In the second place, the suggestion gives due weight to the close analogy between the physical processes involved in vision and hearing respectively. It may be a shock to concede that all the things which we usually say we see have to be inferred from patterns of light that we do not usually say we see. But the evidence in favor of this position is very strong.

CHAPTER FOUR

Auditory Sensations

The conclusion of the last chapter was that through the sense of sight we directly perceive only patterns of light, corresponding to the patterns of sound we directly perceive through the sense of hearing. But the precise nature of the experienced patterns of light was not explained. They were indeed compared with the patterns of sound that we experience in hearing. But this is helpful only if we already understand the true nature of the experienced sounds.

THE NATURE OF SOUNDS HEARD

There does not initially seem to be any great problem about the nature of the sounds we hear. In everyday life, we think of the sounds we hear as public phenomena in the world outside us, accessible in principle to a variety of observers. Different people may hear precisely the same sound. When the referee blows his whistle, everyone hears the same noise.

We may, however, begin to feel doubts about the correctness of this commonsense way of thinking about the sounds we hear once we understand the nature of the physical processes that are involved. According to the physicist, sounds are *wave motions,* propagated in all directions from a source of vibration, such as the vibrating string in a musical instrument.

The vibration of the string is communicated to the particles of matter in the immediate vicinity, which in turn affect other particles, and so on. Ultimately the original vibration of the string may be transmitted over considerable distances by a kind of chain reaction. Since these physical processes are the relevant ones that go on in the world outside us when we hear the sound of a violin, for instance, the question of whether the sounds we directly perceive are public phenomena can be reformulated as the question of whether these sounds are identical with the sound waves described by the physicist. When the question is phrased in this way, there is a natural reluctance to accept the identity of the sounds heard and the sound waves, even though this involves rejecting the commonsense view that the sounds heard are public phenomena. If we are to hear a sound, it is essential that the sound waves emitted by the source strike the ear. It seems much more reasonable to suggest that the sounds directly perceived are sensations of some sort produced in the observer when the sound waves strike the ear.

It is not necessary, however, to decide this question simply on the basis of what appears most reasonable. There is a test available which will determine conclusively whether or not the sounds heard are identical with the sound waves. If they are, the two items will be correlated in such a way that whenever we experience similar sounds, the physicist will detect similar sound waves; and whenever we experience different sounds, the physicist will detect different sound waves. Now, there is certainly some correlation between the sounds we hear and the sound waves measured by the physicist. For example, when a certain piano key is depressed, we hear the musical tone that we call middle C and the physicist detects a sound wave with a frequency of 256 cycles per second. When the key on the immediate right is depressed, we hear the slightly higher musical tone which we call D, and the physicist detects a sound wave with the slightly higher frequency of 280 cycles per second. Even exact correlations, however, are not necessarily due to the *identity* of the sounds we hear and the sound waves produced. There is the alternative theory that the correlations are due to causal connections. Perhaps the sounds heard correlate with the sound waves, not because the two are identical, but because the sounds heard are caused by the sound waves. We can make a decision between the causal theory and the identity theory if we can discover any cases in which there is a breakdown in the usual correlation between experienced sounds and sound waves. Any such discrepancies will directly conflict with the identity theory and will eliminate it. On the other hand, the causal theory can easily explain cases in which the usual correspondence does not occur. Such cases will be due to extraordinary factors interfering with the usual effect produced by the sound waves.

THE DOPPLER EFFECT

There is in fact no shortage of examples to contradict the identity theory and to support the view that the sounds heard are effects produced by the sound waves. One particularly striking example of a change in the sound heard without any corresponding change in the sound wave is provided by the phenomenon known as the *Doppler effect*. This effect, familiar to anyone who has ever heard an airplane passing overhead, occurs whenever there is a relative motion between the observer and the source of the sound. When the observer and the source are coming together, the pitch of the note heard is higher than it is when they are moving apart. The explanation is that when the source and the observer are moving closer together, successive crests of the wave emitted strike the ear of the observer more frequently than they do when the source and the observer are moving apart. When the Doppler effect is produced by the source moving through the transmitting medium, then the change in the sound heard can indeed be explained by a difference in the sound waves involved. The sound waves that a moving object throws out in front of it are different from the sound waves that trail behind it. But the Doppler effect is also produced when the source of the sound is stationary and the observer is moving. In this kind of case the sound wave is radiated evenly in all directions and hence cannot be identified with the sound heard, which changes quite dramatically when the moving observer passes the source. The sound heard is an effect determined by the frequency with which successive crests of the sound wave impinge on the ear of the listener, and this is affected by the motion of the observer as well as by the intrinsic character of the sound wave.

OTHER EXAMPLES

Another example which is less spectacular but just as effective is provided by the testimony of those who are slightly deaf in one ear. Although the pattern of sound waves reaching the observer is constant, the sound heard when the deaf ear is covered and the normal ear uncovered is louder and clearer than the sound heard when the normal ear is covered and the deaf ear uncovered. The sounds heard differ, although the sound waves remain the same, so that the sounds heard cannot be identified with the sound waves. The sounds heard are effects produced by the sound waves, and the nature of the sounds heard is also affected by other factors such as the condition of the ears.

This distinction between the sounds that we directly experience and the sound waves that produce them provides an explanation of the cases in which we seem to be hearing a certain sort of sound, although no sound waves of an appropriate kind can be detected in the immediate vicinity. For example, we sometimes hear what we call a "ringing in the ears." But no sound waves can be found of the sort produced by the ringing of a bell. The explanation is that the ringing sound we hear is merely an auditory sensation. Unlike most of the auditory sensations that we experience, this sensation is not produced by sound waves striking the eardrum. The causes of the sensation lie inside the body.

Another phenomenon which is now totally intelligible is the celebrated paradox of the "sound of silence." Although hard to get in this modern world, we have all had at some time or other the experience of total quietness. We listen intently and we hear nothing. But do we really hear nothing? Must we not admit that in cases like this our auditory experience does have a certain characteristic content which is the sound of silence? This sound of silence which we certainly hear cannot be identified with sound waves, for there are no sound waves. It is an auditory sensation—the sensation which we normally experience in the absence of auditory stimulation.

SOUNDS AS SENSATIONS: THE ANALOGY WITH PAIN

In introducing the idea that the sounds we hear are actually auditory sensations, I am going beyond the original conclusion that the experienced sounds are effects produced in us by sound waves striking the ear. One may indeed wonder what these effects might be if they are not sensations, but the use of the term *sensation* involves an implicit comparison of the heard sounds to pains, tickles, itches, and other sensations with which we are already familiar. This comparison should be justified. I now wish to argue that the implicit comparison of experienced sounds to sensations such as pain is not only legitimate but also very revealing. It is legitimate because the sense of pain has the same basic structure as the sense of hearing. It is revealing because our ordinary ways of thinking and talking about pain display the true structure of this sense, whereas the parallel structure of the other senses is discovered only by philosophical argument. The sense of pain, therefore, supplies us with a familiar model in terms of which we can understand the true nature of all our perceptual experiences.

In the case of the sense of pain, there is no problem about what we directly perceive—the pains themselves. There is surely nothing else from which we infer the pains we say we feel. But what corresponds in the case of pain to the physical things which are the *indirect* objects of perception in other cases? The indirect object of the sense of hearing is a physical thing which causes and is inferred from the sound directly perceived. Therefore, an indirect object of the sense of pain would have to be a physical thing which causes and is inferred from the pain directly perceived. There are certainly many things that do indeed satisfy these criteria. Suppose my finger is pricked by a pin, and I feel a sharp pain. The pin is the cause of the pain that I feel, and I may very well be able to infer the pin from the pain. Suppose I am walking in the woods and feel a sudden pain in my arm. I may be able to infer from the pain the mosquito that is responsible. But is it proper to say that I perceive the pin and the mosquito? If I detect the presence of a man lurking behind a tree by observing the shadow that he casts on the ground, the man behind the tree is the cause of what I see and can be inferred from what I see, but I would nevertheless be reluctant to claim that I saw the man behind the tree. Should I be equally reluctant to claim that I perceived the pin and the mosquito? In everyday life, at any rate, we have no scruples about this. It is just as good English to say that I felt a pin or a mosquito as it is to say that I felt a pain. I can say quite properly that I feel a mosquito when I really feel only the pain. I do not have to reserve this expression for the rare cases when I feel the mosquito before I feel the pain, as when a heavy mosquito makes a clumsy landing.

Thus, the sense of pain and the sense of hearing have the same fundamental structure. In both cases, there are indirect objects of perception that are really inferred from the items directly perceived. When we hear a dog and feel a mosquito, the dog and the mosquito are indirect objects of perception whose presence we infer from the sound we hear and the pain we feel. At the level of commonsense, it does indeed appear that there is one important difference between the two cases. The sounds heard seem to be public phenomena whereas the pains felt are definitely private to the persons by whom they are experienced. When two people are hurt by an explosion, each feels his own private pain, but both heard the same public bang. However, the distinction drawn between the experienced sounds and the sound waves has completely undermined this position. Like the pain I feel when the mosquito bites, the noise I hear when the dog barks is also an effect produced in me by the creature concerned. The sounds I actually hear are as private as the pains I feel. There are therefore good reasons for grouping together the experienced sounds and the experienced pains and calling them sensations. The way in which we actually do talk about our knowledge of the world through the sense of pain provides us with the language in terms of which we should talk about our knowledge of the world through the sense of hearing.

DIFFERENCES BETWEEN PAINS AND SOUNDS

If, in fact, we ought to think about the sense of hearing and the sense of pain in the same way, why do we not do this naturally, without any prodding from philosophers? One real difference between the sense of hearing and the sense of pain is that in the case of hearing, it is always the same part of the body that is affected, namely the ear and auditory system. In the case of pain, on the other hand, different parts of the body may be involved on different occasions. A prick on the finger affects the nerves in the finger; a prick on the toe affects the nerves in the toe. I believe that it is this difference that is largely responsible for our tendency to believe that the sounds we hear are public and that the pains we feel are private in character. Since it is possible, and obviously important, to differentiate our pains in accordance with the particular part of the body affected, we locate the pains we feel in various parts of our body. Once this is done, it is impossible to think of our pains as items lying outside the body in the public domain. On the other hand, although the sounds we hear are just as much effects produced in us as are the pains produced by pins and mosquitoes, there is no variety in the location of these effects. Because of the lack of contrast, we are not even aware that the sounds we hear are bodily sensations. When we do try to locate the sounds we hear, we are understandably concerned with what does vary from case to case — the direction from which the sound waves are coming. After all, it is the location of the source of the sound which is of practical importance for most ordinary purposes. Hence, it is very natural that we should locate the sounds we hear outside the body and thus fail to realize that they are mere auditory sensations.

The practice of locating the sounds heard outside the body is reinforced by the fact that there really are objective phenomena outside the body with which the sounds heard may be (mistakenly) identified. In the case of pain, there is nothing which corresponds to the sound waves connected with hearing, so that any attempt to externalize the pains we feel would be completely unworkable. The externalization of the sounds we hear is by no means unworkable. Although it is strictly the causes of the sounds we hear that are the objective phenomena, the assimilation of the experienced sounds to their external causes leads to few difficulties in practice. One difficulty which does exist, actually, is the problem of explaining auditory hallucinations, when we hear a noise not produced by an external source. This problem is handled in our ordinary thinking by distinguishing *imaginary* sounds, which are purely subjective, from the real, objective sounds which we hear most of the time. This distinction works well enough in practice, even if unsatisfactory from a systematic point of view.

Without conceding that it is anything but a mistake to suppose that the sounds we actually experience are objective phenomena, I have tried to explain why it is natural to make this mistake. We do not make the same mistake in the case of pains, where circumstances do not conspire to mislead us. Therefore, it is our ordinary way of talking about the sense of pain that supplies us with the proper model in terms of which to understand sense perception in general.

Since pains are the most dramatic sensations that we experience, it is natural enough to use the sense of pain as the model for sense perception in general. It would be possible, however, to use other sensations instead. When a feather tickles my face, I may say that I feel the feather, but it is clear that what I really feel is only the tickle, which is a sensation produced in me by the feather brushing my face. Similarly, when the hot sun blazes down on my unprotected neck, I may say that I feel the sun on the back of my neck. But it is quite clear that what I really feel is no more than a certain sensation of heat produced in me by the rays of the sun striking my neck. Although I may think of myself as perceiving the feather and the sun, both objects are actually inferred from the sensations which they produce in me.

CHAPTER FIVE

Visual
Sensations

In Chapter Three, I argued that in visual perception what we directly perceive is a pattern of light, corresponding to the pattern of sound that we directly perceive in the case of hearing. We have now seen that the sounds directly experienced are auditory sensations—effects produced in the observer by sound waves striking the ear. Should we go on to draw the conclusion that the pattern of light directly experienced is a complex of sensations produced in the observer by light waves striking the eye? If the argument up to this point is sound, an affirmative answer to this question is, I believe. inevitable.

In the case of hearing, the key question was whether or not the sounds directly experienced could be identified with the sound waves detected by physical scientists. In the case of vision, there is an exactly similar question about the nature of the experienced patterns of light. Scientists have established the existence of electromagnetic radiations of certain wavelengths which are focused on the retina of the eye and are known as *light waves*. Are the patterns of light directly perceived to be identified with these light waves?

LIGHT WAVES AND VISUAL SENSATIONS

There is certainly a close correlation between the pattern of light waves striking the eye and the pattern of light directly experienced. If the wavelength of the light striking the eye is 440 millimicrons, we see violet; if the wavelength is 680 millimicrons, we see red. Indeed, the correlation between what we experience and the light entering the eye is much closer than the correlation between what we experience and the surface from which the light has been reflected. The pattern of light falling on the retina depends not only on the nature of the surface concerned but also on such things as the inclination of the surface, its distance from the perceiver, and the nature of the medium through which the light passes. The pattern of light experienced is also influenced by these same factors. For example, as I move toward a distant mountain, the mountain itself does not change but there are slow changes both in the light entering my eyes and in the nature of my visual experience.

The close correlation between the pattern of light waves striking the eye and the pattern of light directly perceived may tempt us to identify these items, but we must remember that no matter how precise a correlation is established, the correlation may be explained by a causal relation between the items involved. That is, it may be that the patterns of light directly experienced are *effects* of the patterns of light waves falling on the eye.

As in the case of sound, the evidence that there is no more than a causal relation between the light waves and the pattern actually experienced is provided by cases in which the usual correlation between the two items breaks down. There are discrepancies that reveal that the pattern of light seen is merely an effect caused by the impingement of light waves on the eye. These light waves, moreover, constitute only one of the factors contributing to the effect, even if, in normal cases, they are the most significant factor.

The most striking example of such discrepancies is perhaps the phenomenon of color blindness. Some people are so constituted that they cannot distinguish the colors distinguished by normal observers; most commonly, they cannot distinguish among red, yellow, and green. Suppose that we have two sources of light emitting wavelengths of 520 and 700 millimicrons. The normal observer sees two different colors. But the person who is red-green color blind sees only one color. The point emerges in a particularly dramatic way in the rare cases in which only one eye is color blind. When such observers use the right eye, they see a different pattern of colors from the pattern of colors they see when they use the left eye. And yet, the nature of the light affecting both eyes is presumably the same. This means that the pattern of light seen cannot be identified with the light waves that affect the eye. Factors such as the physical condition of the eye have an effect on the pattern of colors seen but obviously have no effect on the constitution of the light that comes to the eye.

EXPERIENCED ITEMS ARE ALL
OF THE SAME KIND

This argument to show that the pattern of light experienced is not identical with the light waves striking the eye does indeed depend on a certain assumption—the assumption that the items directly experienced are all of the same kind. There is a similar assumption lying at the back of the earlier argument that distinguished between the sounds heard and the sound waves. All that has been strictly established is that not all the experienced visual patterns can be identified with patterns of light falling on the retina. In the case of the man who is color blind in one eye, since what he sees with his left eye is different from what he sees with his right eye, we cannot identify both visual patterns with the pattern of light waves entering the eyes. But it is theoretically possible that one of the visual patterns is identical with the light waves. This is, however, a theoretical possibility which need not be taken very seriously. The suggestion is that on some occasions we are directly aware of the light waves themselves, whereas on other occasions we are merely aware of effects produced in us by the light waves. This is unlikely in the extreme. It is much more reasonable to suppose that in visual perception we are always directly aware of mere visual sensations, the discrepancies between what we see and the light waves being due to the influence of the other factors which contribute to the formation of the visual sensations.

INTERNALLY PRODUCED VISUAL
SENSATIONS

We have already seen that pains and auditory sensations are not always produced by external stimuli. Sometimes, the causes of these sensations lie within the percipient organism itself. If it is true that the direct objects of visual experience are visual sensations, it may reasonably be expected that there will also be visual sensations that are not produced by light waves striking the eye. I shall use an example which is so obvious that it usually escapes notice.

Suppose that I go into a pitch black room— a room so dark that there are absolutely no light waves striking my eyes. What do I see? Certainly not light waves, since there are no light waves. There may be a sense in which I can see nothing, in so far as I cannot make out even the contours of any object in the room. But it is equally clear that I am not totally without visual experience, in the way in which the congenitally blind may be without visual experience. I am aware of something, and something that I can describe. Even if I were merely aware of simple undifferentiated blackness, that would still be something. In actual fact I am aware of something rather more complex than this. I am aware of a dark field studded with pinpoints of light. But what is this dark field? It is not a complex of surfaces, and it is not a complex of light waves. It has no existence in the external world, nor is it even generated by what exists in the external world. It must be some sort of sensation that has its origin in the perceiver him- or herself. It must be the visual sensation that the perceiver enjoys when no light is affecting the retina. (This example is, of course, the counterpart from the sense of sight to the "sound of silence" example in the previous chapter.)

It is worth noticing that the change in the visual sensation following stimulation of the retina does not totally obliterate the visual pattern experienced in the dark. The pinpoints of light can be dimly discerned as an ingredient in the total experience, even if our attention is normally focused on the differentiation of areas of color. This retention of the visual pattern experienced in the dark as a component in our ordinary visual experience provides additional confirmation for a theory that does not make a radical distinction between what is directly perceived in the dark and what is directly perceived when light falls upon the retina. In both cases, what is directly perceived is nothing but a visual sensation. When it is dark, all that we can infer from our visual sensation is that it is dark. When it is not dark, we can infer the specific character of the physical objects in the vicinity from the specific character of the visual sensation.

HALLUCINATIONS

Another type of case in which we experience visual sensations not produced by light striking the eye is less common but more spectacular.

Although visual hallucinations are comparatively rare phenomena, they do occur from time to time, especially if people are shut up in dark caves for weeks on end or indulge to excess in alcoholic beverages. Perhaps the most famous example of a hallucination is the dagger seen by Macbeth before the murder of Duncan. Macbeth experienced exactly the visual sensation he would have experienced had his eyes been affected by light waves reflected from the surface of a real dagger. He was tempted to suppose that there was indeed a dagger before him. Noticing, however, that the dagger was an impalpable dagger which could not be clutched, he comes to the conclusion that it is but "A dagger of the mind, a false creation/Proceeding from the heat-oppressed brain" (*Macbeth*, Act II, Scene I 38-39).

There is an important difference between hallucinations and illusions. In the case of a visual illusion, the pattern of colors that we see can be attributed to the pattern of light waves affecting the eye. The optical illusion is due to the fact that these light waves have had an abnormal history. For example, when we look at a mirror, we have the illusion of seeing a world of objects through the looking glass. But we all know that the objects we see are not really on the other side of the glass. The explanation of the illusion is that the light waves reflected from the objects do not enter the eyes directly, as they usually do, but only after being reflected a second time by the mirror surface. In the case of a hallucination, however, the pattern of colors of which the subject is aware cannot be attributed to a pattern of light waves affecting the eye. There is no pattern of light waves of an appropriate kind, and in the case of the person in a dark cave, no light waves at all.

VISUAL IMAGES

I have been explaining hallucinations, using the technical concept of *visual sensation* which I have introduced. It may be suggested that a more natural explanation could be given, using the ordinary notion of a *visual image*. We are all familiar with the visual images that usually come unbidden in both dreams and waking life, although we may also form visual images deliberately in accordance with previous specifications. On demand, I can form a visual image of the Taj Mahal, even if somewhat fuzzy. There is indeed a certain similarity between visual images and what we see when observing the physical world. There must be—otherwise, how would we recognize a visual image that pops into mind as, say, the visual image of a dog? But usually, there is a faintness and vagueness and lack of vivacity about our visual images that allows us to tell when we are forming an image and when we are seeing the real thing. Sometimes, however, a visual image attains such a degree of vividness and detail that it cannot be distinguished from what is experienced in the case of genuine perception. This is what happens in hallucinations. The drunkard can detect no difference between what he is experiencing and what he would be experiencing were he seeing a real pink elephant. If he realizes that he is suffering from a hallucination, it is only because he knows that there are no such things as pink elephants and that even if there were, they would not suddenly materialize out of thin air.

VISUAL IMAGES AND VISUAL SENSATIONS

I have already argued that what we directly perceive when we look at a physical object is a visual sensation produced in us by light coming from the physical object. At the level of commonsense, it is natural to suppose that the visual image of a cow actually resembles the animal grazing in the field. But we can now understand that the direct comparison is between the image and the visual sensation produced by light reflected from the surface of the cow. In the case of a hallucination, what we cannot distinguish is the visual image and the visual sensation which would have been produced by a real object of the appropriate kind. That is, visual images may be so like visual sensations that we cannot tell which is which. But how can these things be exactly alike unless they are items of the same fundamental type? If we like, we may call items of this type *visual sensations* when they are generated by light striking the eye, and *visual images* when they have a purely internal origin. But it is also legitimate to emphasize the fundamental similarity by treating visual images as a subset of the class of visual sensations, in a wide sense which includes items of this type whatever their origin.

I shall continue to use the notion of visual sensation as the central concept in my theory, thus emphasizing the analogy between visual experience and the experience of pains, tickles, and so on. It must not be forgotten, however, that there is available in the resources of ordinary language this distinct and alternative concept of a visual image. At the moment, I am using the concept of sensation without attempting to probe too deeply into the nature of the items it designates. Nevertheless, the nature of sensation is obviously a legitimate and important topic; and in any attempt to elucidate this topic, the alternative concept of a mental image may well prove invaluable.

CHAPTER SIX

Visual Perception

INFERENCE FROM VISUAL SENSATIONS

It is now time to draw together the theory of visual perception that I have been developing. According to this theory, the direct objects of visual experience are always visual sensations (understanding this term in a broad sense to include visual images). Usually, but not always, the visual sensations are produced by light falling on the retina of the eye. Sometimes, the light which reaches the eye comes directly from its source, but more often it is reflected or deflected en route. From the visual sensations directly perceived, it is possible to make inferences about the character of the external world involved in their production. We sometimes infer the nature and position of the source of light; we sometimes infer the nature and position of surfaces and objects from which light has been reflected. From time to time, we make other inferences from the visual sensations that cannot be strictly classified under either of the above headings. For example, we may infer the shadow cast by an object, and we may infer the presence of mist and fog. Thus, we are actually inferring from the visual sensations directly perceived things that we say we see in everyday life. We may say that we see a star, which is a source of light. We may say that we see a table, or some surface of a table, from which light has been reflected. We may say that we see shadows and that we see mist and fog. All these things, however, are merely *indirect* objects of perception which are inferred from the visual sensations directly experienced.

ERRORS OF VISUAL PERCEPTION

The inferences that we make from visual sensations usually prove to be fairly reliable, but they are by no means completely foolproof. There are a number of things that can go wrong. The most radical errors occur when we suppose that a visual sensation is produced by light falling on the retina, when the sensation is really of internal origin. When Macbeth thought he saw a dagger, he was suffering from this kind of hallucination. His visual sensation was produced by the "heat-oppressed brain." Even when the visual sensations really are produced by external stimuli, we may still make mistakes. Basically, the source of these mistakes is that the same visual sensation may be produced in different ways. Mistakes are made when we suppose that visual sensations are produced in one way when they are really produced in some other way. This is a particular problem when the cause of a sensation is abnormal or unusual. We fall into error because we naturally assume that the sensation is produced in the usual way with which we are familiar. For example, we may suppose that we can see two stars when there is really only one, because we are seeing double. We are misled because the visual sensation that we experience is just like the visual sensation usually experienced when two stars are affecting the retina. In this case, the source of the mistake lies in the visual apparatus itself. Because of the condition of the visual system, the pattern of light falling on the eye has produced a visual sensation different from that which it would normally produce and similar to that which would normally be produced by a quite different pattern of light.

In other cases, the source of the problem is that the same pattern of light may be generated in different ways. For example, the pattern of light reflected from a mirror is just like the pattern of light which would come from a set of objects on the other side of the glass. We may be deceived, especially when the cues that normally allow us to detect the presence of a mirror are removed. Also, the pattern of light reaching the eye from a large object at a great distance, such as the sun, may be similar to the pattern of light reaching the eye from a smaller object not so far away, such as the moon. Therefore, in certain circumstances, we may easily make mistakes when estimating the size and distance of the things we see. It is only through considerable practice and through the ingenious use of ancillary information that we are able to do as well as we do.

Mistakes in perception are particularly common when conditions of observation are far from ideal. For example, I may suppose that the dim shape that I see through the fog is a man in a black cape waiting to pounce, when it is really only a bush. This is because objects that normally produce quite different visual sensations in an observer may produce very similar sensations when the conditions of observation are below standard (e.g., when the objects are seen through a fog or at a great distance). Just as we can correct mistakes in perception by improving on conditions of observation that are below standard, so we can also correct perceptual mistakes by improving even on standard conditions through the use of various optical instruments such as the microscope and the telescope. We have just seen that things that produce different visual sensations in standard conditions may produce similar sensations when the conditions of observation are *below* standard. It is now clear that things which produce similar visual sensations in standard conditions may produce different sensations when the conditions of observation are *above* standard. In the first case, we are unable to discriminate visually between things that we can normally distinguish; in the second case, we are able to discriminate visually between things that we cannot normally distinguish. For example, a detective may suppose that the red pool on the floor beside the body is blood. The forensic scientist who examines the substance through the microscope will be able to correct the detective's mistake. When viewed with the naked eye, the red substance produces the same visual sensations as blood. When viewed through a microscope, it does not: it looks more like tomato paste.

NAIVE REALISM

The theory that in visual perception we are directly aware of only visual sensations produced in us by light affecting the eyes is in radical opposition to what appears to be our ordinary commonsense way of thinking about visual perception. The commonsense view, to which philosophers usually give the not very complimentary name of *naive realism,* is somewhat elusive, because it is an unstable position which tends to disintegrate under the scrutiny necessary to state it precisely and explicitly. Basically, the idea is that it is the external objects themselves that are directly present in visual experience, and not mere sensations which represent them. The eye is regarded as a kind of peephole in the head through which we look out at the external world. Through this peephole we can observe no more than a limited portion of the world at any one time. However, the peephole can be moved by moving the head, and we can see what we want by getting into a suitable position. The important point is that through this peephole we directly perceive the real physical world and not some representation which interposes itself between the observer and the world.

THE ANALOGY WITH TELEVISION

According to the theory that I have been proposing, the eye is not a peephole: it is more like a camera. In the pupil of the eye, there is a lens, much like the lens in a camera, which focuses the light rays and directs them on to the retina. If we want an analogy for the whole process, perhaps the most appropriate one is that of closed circuit television. The retina is sensitive to light in much the same way as the structure at the back of a television camera. When light falls on the retina, certain changes take place that cause nerve impulses to pass along the optic nerve. This may be compared to electrical impulses passing along the cables of a closed circuit television system. We may then compare the brain cells that are excited by the nerve impulses coming from the retina to a television receiver, and the sensations directly perceived to the picture projected on the screen.

This analogy is genuinely helpful because it provides us with a familiar instance of a situation in which one thing represents something else because of a complicated causal process connecting the two items. The picture that appears on the screen of a television set is a very different kind of thing from the physical objects that come within the field of view of the television camera. Nevertheless, because of the causal processes involved in its production, what appears on the screen may be regarded as a representation of the physical objects concerned. Similarly, although visual sensations are very different in nature from physical objects, we may think of the visual sensations as representing the external causes by which they have been produced.

The analogy with television should not, of course, be pressed too far. Like most analogies, it is not exact in every respect. For example, we must not be misled into supposing that the visual sensation, like the picture on the screen, is a two-dimensional representation of a three-dimensional reality. Whatever the visual sensation may be, it is not a flat two-dimensional picture. Due to the binocular nature of the visual system, we find in immediate experience a certain element of depth.

Nor does the visual sensation represent the external objects in quite the same way as a television picture represents the scene that it depicts. Although the surface of the television screen is different in many ways from the system of objects in front of the television camera, there is an important similarity, since both things emit similar patterns of light waves and hence produce similar visual sensations in the minds of observers. We certainly cannot use this model to explain the similarity between visual sensations and the external objects they represent. But the visual sensations must represent physical objects in some sense, if we are to be able to make inferences from the nature of the sensations to the nature of the physical things that have produced these sensations.

INADEQUACIES OF NAIVE REALISM

The theory that we are directly aware of only visual sensations that are caused by and represent the physical objects in the field of view is sometimes called the *causal representative theory*. This theory appears to be a great advance on the theory of naive realism. Naive realism cannot handle the discrepancies between what we actually experience and what we believe to exist in the physical world. Curiously enough, the naive realist can deal most successfully with the most extreme discrepancies such as total hallucinations. Here it may be said that what is actually experienced is a vivid mental image that the subject may mistake for the real thing. We are not, indeed, provided with an explanation of how a mere image can counterfeit so successfully a real physical object, but the account we are offered is by no means implausible.

It is the more modest discrepancies between what we see and what is there that ensure the collapse of naive realism. For example, the naive realist cannot give a satisfactory explanation of the famous illusion of the straight stick that appears bent when half-immersed in water. It can hardly be seriously suggested that we are seeing the real stick before it is placed in the water when an image that misrepresents the physical reality is suddenly substituted. The naive realist has an even greater difficulty in explaining the changes in what we see that accompany changes in the position of the object under observation. When a plane takes off and flies away into the distance, what we see gets smaller and smaller, although the real plane does not get any smaller. This is easily explained if we acknowledge that what is directly perceived is only a visual sensation produced by light reflected from the surface of the plane. It cannot be explained if we insist that we are directly perceiving what is really there.

Another disadvantage of naive realism is that it must ignore completely the scientific evidence concerning the physical processes involved in perception—scientific evidence that is incorporated in an appropriate way by the causal representative theory. Once we understand the nature of the physical processes that intervene in visual perception between the observer and the external object, it is difficult to take seriously the naive realist claim that it is the external object itself that is directly perceived and not some effect that it produces in the observer by reflecting light that falls on the retina.

TIME LAG ARGUMENT

One point about the physical processes involved in perception which is particularly relevant to the present issue is that these are processes that take time to complete. Since light travels at such a high speed, the time that elapses between the emission or reflection of light and the effect on the retina is usually incredibly small. However, in the case of the most distant objects we can perceive, the time involved may be very considerable. When we look at a distant star, the light that is reaching the eye was emitted many years ago. Indeed, the star which we say we see may no longer exist. It may have been blown to bits in some cosmic catastrophe at the time of the American Revolution. Although this is an extreme case, in every case the event or state of an object involved in the emission or reflection of light is already in the past by the time the light arrives at the retina. This means that by the time we enjoy the visual experience, the event or state that is causally responsible does not exist. But what is directly experienced certainly does exist and is contemporary with the experience. Therefore, what is directly perceived cannot be the external state or event that originated the physical process. We cannot directly perceive what is in the past and no longer exists. The time lag between the emission of light and the visual experience is most significant in the case of the distant star, but if this is accepted we must also accept smaller time lags when light is emitted by the sun, reflected by the moon, reflected by a distant mountain, or reflected by the table in front of our eyes. *Any* time lag is incompatible with the naive realist theory that we directly perceive external objects. On the other hand, a time lag between the original emission of light and the appearance of the visual sensation directly perceived is precisely what a supporter of the causal representative theory would expect.

THE SCIENTIFIC EVIDENCE

The way in which the causal representative theory incorporates the scientific evidence relates to the earlier point about this theory's explanation for the discrepancy between what is directly experienced and what exists in the physical world. Indeed, we must appeal to the scientific evidence in order to explain in detail those changes in what is directly experienced that are not accompanied by changes in the physical objects that we say we see. The visual sensations directly experienced are not produced simply by the external objects we say we see. There are various conditions of observation which also make a contribution to the character of the sensation experienced. A change in any of these conditions of observation may bring about a change in the experienced sensation, even if the external object principally concerned remains unchanged. For example, the change in what is experienced when a stick is half immersed in water is due to a change in the medium intervening between the stick and the eye, not to a change in the stick itself. This is one of the conditions of observation that contribute to the nature of the experienced sensation. What factor is responsible when the visual sensation changes without any change in the external object proper must be tracked down in each particular case by examining the physical processes recognized in a scientific study of perception.

EXPERIENCED SENSATIONS
AND PHYSIOLOGICAL PROCESSES

Although the causal representative theory ties in very closely with what the physicist and the physiologist have to say about the physical processes involved in perception, the theory as such is a philosophical rather than a scientific theory. The theory introduces an experiential item—the perceived sensation—that does not and cannot appear in the account of perceptual processes given by the physiologist. The physiologist details chemical processes in the retina, nerve impulses passing along the optic nerve, and electrical activity in various parts of the brain, but he or she never mentions the experienced sensations as such.

This brings in another problem which I have been careful to avoid until now. What is the precise relation between the visual sensations directly experienced and the various processes studied by the physiologist? In Chapter Five, I argued that the visual patterns directly experienced could not be identified with the patterns of light waves striking the eye but were effects produced in the observer by light falling on the retina. The various processes that the physiologist detects in the optic nerve and the visual cortex are also effects produced in the observer by light falling on the retina. Should we identify the experienced visual patterns with these physiological processes?

We were able to defeat the attempt to identify the visual pattern with the light falling on the retina by producing cases in which the items experienced were different although the light waves striking the retina were the same. It is harder to drive this kind of a wedge between the experienced pattern and at least some of the processes that figure in the physiological account. But even if we cannot produce any cases in which we have different experienced patterns and similar physiological processes, this does not establish the identity of the visual patterns and the physiological processes that correspond to them. Even a perfect correlation may be due to a causal connection rather than the identity of the items correlated.

The question of the relation between the visual sensations and the corresponding physiological processes is an extremely tricky question which I shall not attempt to answer at the present time. It is a special case of the fundamental puzzle about the relation of mind and body which has worried philosophers since the days of ancient Greece without yielding an agreed-upon solution. This means that for the time being, we will have to work with a concept of visual sensation that is not fully integrated with what we know about the physical processes occurring in the optic nerve and the visual cortex. We must assume that the visual sensations are effects produced in us by light striking the eye without being able to explain the sense in which these sensations are "in us." But although we must postpone the satisfaction of the very natural ambition to provide a comprehensive theory that will integrate our immediate experience and our physiological knowledge, it is better to leave a question unsettled than to risk settling it in the wrong way by a premature synthesis.

CHAPTER SEVEN

Visual Appearances

If the direct objects of visual perception are always visual sensations from which we have to infer the surfaces, shadows, rainbows, tables, chairs, and all the other things that we say we see, why do we never come across references to these visual sensations in everyday language? Granted, there are reasons for being more interested in the nature of the physical-objects in the vicinity than in the nature of our sensations. Because of this interest, it is more common for people to talk about hearing dogs, trains, burglars, and so on than to talk about hearing sounds and noises. But we do sometimes say we hear sounds and noises. Why, then, do we never refer in everyday language to visual sensations? In the case of hearing, there are circumstances in which a reference to sounds and noises cannot be avoided. It is essential to refer to sounds and noises directly perceived in order to explain the mistakes that we sometimes make when inferring the source of the sound. If I suppose that I am hearing a dog when it is really only a person imitating a dog, I have to explain my mistake by pointing out that the sound I heard was very like sounds usually made by dogs. Now, we sometimes make similar mistakes in the case of visual perception. For example, I may suppose that I am seeing a flock of sheep on a distant hillside, when it is really only a group of white boulders. Using the notion of visual sensation, I can explain my mistake by pointing out that at such a distance a flock of sheep and a group of white boulders will produce in the observer very similar visual sensations, so that the possibility of confusion is quite understandable. But how can we explain such mistakes in everyday language in which the notion of visual sensation is not used?

LANGUAGE OF APPEARANCE

The answer is, of course, that we give the required explanation by using the notion of *appearing* or *looking*. Instead of saying that the flock of sheep and the group of boulders produce similar sensations in a distant observer, we say that a flock of sheep and a group of boulders look similar when viewed from a distance. Perceptual errors are possible because different things may look similar and similar things may look different. That is, in everyday language, we explain our mistakes by talking about how things look or appear, instead of introducing visual sensations.

In everyday life, when I say that something looks red, this is often because I think that the thing is red, but I am not quite sure. If I had been quite sure, I would have asserted categorically that the thing was red. This may lead one to suppose that the statement that a thing *looks* red is equivalent to a tentative judgment that the thing *is* red. This is a complete mistake. It is perfectly proper to say that a thing looks red, if it does, even when one knows very well that the thing is not really red at all. Also, it is perfectly correct to say that something looks red, if it does, even when one is completely sure that it not only looks red, but is red. A red flag is red; but it would not fulfill its warning function unless it also looked red to normal observers. A thing may look red, whether or not it really is red; and we may say that it looks red, whatever our views about what it really is.

Although the notion of things looking a certain way gets its meaning for me from situations in which I experience things looking a certain way to *me,* it is possible to use the terminology of looking or appearing with a more objective meaning. In addition to saying simply that this object now looks to me like that object, I may also make general statements to the effect that things of a certain type look like things of another type, either in all standard conditions or in certain specified conditions. For example, I may say that whisky looks like weak tea, or that from the riverbank, a crocodile in the water looks like a floating log. Such "objective" statements, however, although they may abstract from any specific observer, necessarily involve a reference to some standard possible observer. Whisky looks like weak tea because it looks like weak tea to any normal observer. From the riverbank, a crocodile in the water looks like a floating log because it looks like a floating log to any normal observer watching from the bank of the river.

TRANSLATION INTO LANGUAGE
OF VISUAL SENSATION

Any statement made in everyday language using the *look* terminology can be translated into a corresponding statement using the notion of visual sensation. The translation is easy, whether I am talking merely about how something looks to me or making a more objective claim about how something looks to people in general. Because I am near-sighted, to me distant objects look rather blurred. Translated into the language of visual sensation, the point is that distant objects produce in me rather blurred visual sensations. In the same way, if whisky looks like weak tea, then whisky and weak tea produce similar visual sensations in any normal observer. If from the riverbank, a crocodile in the water looks like a floating log, then the crocodile in the water produces in any observer on the riverbank sensations resembling the sensations that would be produced in that observer by a floating log.

If it is as easy as this to translate statements using the notion of *looking* into statements using the notion of *visual sensation,* does it really make all that much difference which of these idioms is employed? When I look at a straight stick half immersed in water, I can describe my experience either by saying that the stick looks bent or by saying that the stick is producing in me visual sensations that resemble the visual sensations normally produced by bent sticks. The second way of speaking is less familiar and more cumbersome, but apart from that, is there any difference? Since both idioms unambiguously pick out precisely the same experience, there is no difference for practical purposes. The difference lies in the theoretical implications of the two ways of talking.

To understand what I am getting at, compare the statement: "The sun rose at 6 A.M." with the statement: "At 6 A.M., the revolution of the earth exposed the sun." There is a sense in which these two statements assert precisely the same empirical fact. But they have different theoretical implications. To talk about the sun rising is to compare the sun to a balloon, rising above the edge of the disk. Scientific investigation has revealed that this is a most misleading analogy. However strange and clumsy the second statement may appear, it is this statement that embodies the superior theory.

SOPHISTICATED REALISM

The choice of this example may suggest that I favor the cumbersome, unfamiliar terminology of visual sensation over the neater idiom used in everyday language. What the example proves, however, is merely that our ordinary ways of talking may be inferior from a theoretical point of view, not that they must be. Indeed, there are philosophers who believe that the account of visual experience that employs the notion of looking or appearing is not only neater and more familiar but also more correct. The use of the notion of a visual appearance makes possible a much more persuasive version of direct realism than the naive realism rejected in the previous chapter. The naive realist can give a plausible explanation of the discrepancies between what we experience and what is there only in the case of complete hallucinations, where it is reasonable to suppose that we have confused a visual image with the real thing. Using the notion of visual appearance, we can deal with the less radical discrepancies that are revealed, for example, whenever we change our position with respect to some external object. When I change my position with respect to an object, there is a change in how the object appears to me that is not accompanied by any change in its intrinsic nature. Since I am aware of the object only as it appears to me, there will be a change in my experience without a corresponding change in the external object.

I shall try to present this more sophisticated version of realism as forcefully as possible, in order to make intelligible the strength of conviction in its supporters and the sort of criticisms that they would make of the theory that I have been developing. The crucial point is that although we are aware of external objects only as they appear to us, this does not preclude us from a direct awareness of these external objects. The causal representative theory of visual perception may be admitted as a genuine advance on naive realism, because it does recognize the presence in experience of the visual appearances, which are ignored by the naive realist. The mistake of the causal representative theory is that it turns the visual appearance into the object directly perceived—an object that interposes itself as a barrier between the observer and the external thing. But the visual appearance is *not* the object of perception: it is how the object appears to the experiencing subject. Visual appearances are not things in their own right: they are merely the ways in which the perceived objects appear to the perceiver. The causal representative theory goes wrong because it takes over uncritically the simple-minded two-term analysis of the basic structure of perceptual experience adopted by the naive realist. Both theories are agreed that perception is a process in which a subject simply contemplates or inspects an object. The naive realist contemplates an external object: he or she sees the table. The supporter of the causal representative theory contemplates an internal object: he or she sees a visual sensation produced by the table. Both theories alike make the mistake of introducing only two terms in their analysis of the fundamental structure of perception—a perceiving subject and a perceived object. A proper analysis requires three terms—the perceiving subject, the perceived object, and a third element that is how the perceived object appears to the perceiving subject. The objects that we directly perceive are the external physical objects, even if we perceive them only as they appear to us.

UNIFIED THEORY IN TERMS OF VISUAL SENSATIONS

This sophisticated version of direct realism is initially a persuasive and attractive position, with a very plausible explanation of the mistakes of competing theories. One problem, however, about treating visual appearances as fundamental components in the universe is that it increases by one the number of distinct categories of elements that must be fitted into any comprehensive account of the nature of things. On the other hand, if visual appearances can be analyzed in terms of visual images or sensations, our general account of the universe will be that much simpler. The notion of visual appearance is well suited for the purpose of explaining the changes in experience that accompany changes in the relative position of the observer and the external object, or optical illusions like the straight stick that appears bent when half immersed in water. But we need the notion of visual image to explain complete hallucinations like Macbeth's dagger, and we need the notion of visual sensation to explain the visual experience we enjoy in total darkness. Thus, only if we are prepared to analyze visual appearances in terms of visual sensations can we provide the unified account of visual experience which is so desirable. Such an analysis has indeed the bonus that it allows us to produce a unified theory that covers not only our visual experience but also our experience of other sensations such as pains.

UNIFIED THEORY IN TERMS
OF APPEARANCES

It may be suggested, however, that a unified account of experience can be supplied from the other side. It may be more natural to explain hallucinations by saying that a vivid visual image has been confused with the real thing, but is it absolutely impossible to provide an explanation in terms of visual appearances? Macbeth's hallucination was that he seemed to see a dagger before him. May we not suggest that what Macbeth actually saw was a certain dagger-shaped region of the air which for special reasons appeared to him like a dagger rather than like the empty air it really was? This suggestion gains confirmation from the fact that there is often something distinctive in the appropriate region that triggers the hallucination. The alcoholic converts the damp stain on the plaster into a loathsome reptile. To him, the stain on the plaster looks like a snake. It is not a particularly radical move to propose a similar explanation, even in cases in which there is no external trigger. The region of space where the hallucinatory object seems to be located, instead of looking the way it does to normal people, looks like a snake or a dagger.

The same sort of explanation can be provided for our experience in total darkness, which originally led us to introduce visual sensations. We experience a dark field permeated by points of light. This is how everything appears in total darkness, just as everything appears as a vague black shape when it is almost dark. It is as proper to say that in the night all cows look black as it is to say that in the day they look the different colors that distinguish the different breeds.

DIFFICULTIES WITH APPEARANCE THEORY

To offer this account of hallucinations and the other cases is indeed to sacrifice one advantage of the idiom of looking and appearing, which is its greater naturalness. It is quite artificial to explain Macbeth's vision in terms of how a certain dagger-shaped region of empty space appeared to Macbeth. A more serious difficulty, however, is that there are some visual experiences that cannot be expressed in terms of how some object appears to the perceiver, no matter how artificial one is prepared to be. Whatever we may say about the extraordinary mental images that are confused with real things in hallucinations, there is no plausible way of representing our ordinary mental images as how some external object appears to the experiencing subject. I close my eyes and form the visual image of a horse. What is it that looks to me like a horse? There is nothing in my experience but the visual image itself.

It is, of course, possible to suggest that the correct explanation of visual perception requires us to introduce both visual images and irreducible visual appearances. It may be simpler to explain everything in terms of visual sensations, but it is difficult to prove that this consideration is conclusive. Perhaps it is the more complex explanation that is correct. However, any theory that introduces visual appearances that cannot be reduced to visual sensations faces the task of explaining the nature of these appearances and their place in the universe. This is a task that must be accomplished whether the visual appearances are introduced instead of or in addition to visual images. The visual appearances depend partly on the nature of the object perceived and partly on the conditions of observation. For example, how the table looks to me depends partly on the nature of the table and partly on the source of light, the relative positions of myself and the table, the character of the intervening medium, the condition of the eye, and so on. This fact about the visual appearance of the table is perfectly intelligible if we explain it in terms of the effect that the table has on the observer in virtue of the light waves emitted by the sun and reflected to the eye. There does not seem to be any alternative explanation of how the visual appearance can be a function of both the external object and the conditions of observation. But if we analyze the visual appearance in terms of the effect that the object has on the observer, this is tantamount to an analysis in terms of visual sensations. Either we reduce visual appearances to visual sensations, or else we leave their functional dependence on both the external objects and the conditions of observation totally unexplained. The causal representative theory may have an unresolved problem about the relationship between the visual sensations and the physiological processes in the nervous system, but whether the visual sensations are identical with or caused by the physiological processes, we have an explanation of why the visual sensations are a function of both the conditions of observation and the external objects that we say we perceive.

WEAKNESSES OF DIRECT REALISM

The problem facing a direct realist who tries to explain how the visual appearances depend on both the external objects and the conditions of observation is simply one facet of a general inability to handle the scientific evidence concerning the physical processes involved in perception. Another illustration of this weakness in direct realism is that it cannot answer the time lag argument. The version of the theory that recognizes visual appearances is no better off than the original naive realism. Neither version of the theory can explain how we can be directly aware of external objects, given that the relevant processes in a distant star occurred many years ago.

A FINAL EXAMPLE

We can illustrate the overall superiority of the causal representative theory in a very convincing way by comparing the following three cases. In the first case, I am watching the sky at night when the moon emerges suddenly from behind a cloud. In the second case, I am lying on my back at the beach. I have my eyes closed, and suddenly the sun comes out from behind a cloud. In the third case, I am also at the beach, but this time I am lying face down when the sun comes out from behind the cloud. Even in the third case, I can easily tell what has happened. I feel a sudden sensation of warmth on my back and infer that the sun is shining again. I do not directly perceive the sun and the cloud, but I infer the objective situation from the sensation that I do experience. The causal representative theory offers the same sort of account in the other two cases. When I am lying on my back, I infer that the sun has appeared from the red glow that is the visual sensation produced in me by sunlight falling on my closed eyelids. In the same way, I do not directly perceive the moon emerging from behind the cloud. Instead, I directly experience only a visual sensation produced by light from the moon falling on the retina: I have to infer the moon that is responsible.

The direct realist can offer an initially plausible alternative explanation of the perception of the moon. He or she can even explain the second case without introducing visual sensations, if he or she is prepared to interpret the red glow we experience as how the sun looks through closed eyes. But the same account cannot be given in all three cases, since the direct realist has to admit sensations of warmth in order to explain how we are able to tell that the sun has come out from behind the cloud when we are lying face down. It is particularly unfortunate that the direct realist cannot tell the same story in all three cases, in view of the fact that the scientific account of the physical processes involved in each case is very similar. In all three cases, a cloud that is intercepting the flow of electromagnetic radiation from the heavenly body to my body moves out of the way. If there is one case in which we directly experience only an effect produced in us by this radiation, it is difficult to suppose that in the other cases we directly experience anything more.

The causal representative theory not only has the advantage of simplicity in that it tells much the same sort of story in every case, but also the story it tells is closely integrated with the scientific account of the physical processes that are going on. Granted, there is still a residual problem of explaining the relation between the experienced sensations and the physiological processes in the nervous system, but this is a small gap compared with the enormous gap that separates the scientist and the direct realist.

In the comparison which I have been exploring, I have been assuming that at least in the case when I am lying face down, I must be making an inference from an experienced sensation of warmth. If this is challenged, it is possible to buttress my argument by the introduction of a fourth case. Let us suppose that someone has been attacked by a gang at the beach. They are holding him face downward in the sand and burning his back with a powerful magnifying glass. The only thing that spoils their fun is that the sun keeps passing behind small clouds, cutting off their source of power. The victim can tell when the sun goes behind a cloud, not because he directly perceives this, but because he can make this inference from the decreased intensity of his sensation of pain. Surely in this case, there is no alternative explanation, and no question of directly perceiving the sun!

CHAPTER EIGHT

The General Theory

THE SENSE OF TASTE

Once it has been conceded that in the case of visual perception we are directly aware of only visual sensations from which we have to infer the various things that we normally say we see, there is likely to be little fight about the same being true for the other senses through which we acquire information about the external world. For example, in the case of the sense of taste, we are not, as we might suppose, directly aware of properties of things that we say have a sweet, sour, salt, or bitter taste. Instead, we are directly aware of only sensations produced in us by things in the mouth affecting the tongue and the palate. We infer the taste properties of these things from the sensations that they produce.

One important line of evidence to which I have appealed in other cases to show that the direct object of perception is a sensation is that there is a variation in what is directly experienced without a corresponding variation in the external object concerned, due to a change in the conditions of observation. There is less scope for this sort of variation in the sense of taste than in the case of visual perception, because the conditions of observation are much less complex. Nevertheless, there are cases where we do find a change in the sensation experienced without any corresponding change in the substance in the mouth. Try this simple experiment. Suck an orange that tastes quite sweet. Then, eat a few spoonfuls of sugar. Next, suck the orange again. It now tastes quite sour. The taste is different, but no one supposes that the orange itself has changed. The result of this experiment becomes intelligible if we admit that the tastes directly experienced are only sensations produced by the orange, not its real qualities. We think of the orange as objectively having a definite taste, only because the orange does have certain definite chemical properties which affect the tongue and the palate, producing in normal circumstances a certain definite sort of sensation. Similar substances with similar chemical properties normally produce similar sensations of taste. This is why we can talk in objective terms about the taste of oranges, the taste of coffee, and the taste of sugar. But there are exceptional cases that make it necessary to distinguish between the objective taste of the substance and the sensation of taste directly experienced. There are other causal factors involved in the production of a sensation in addition to the chemical properties of the substance in the mouth. Any change in these other causal factors may affect the sensation ultimately experienced. In the particular case of the sweet orange that tastes sour, it is clear that the overdose of sugar has affected the organs of taste. In this abnormal situation, the sensation of taste produced is abnormal too.

THE SENSE OF TEMPERATURE

Another sense which lends itself readily to the kind of analysis I have been proposing is the sense of temperature which permits us to gauge roughly how hot or cold things are. We may estimate the general temperature of the air or we may estimate the temperature of specific objects in the vicinity. In the case of this sense, it is particularly difficult to deny that we determine the temperature of external objects on the basis of the sensations of heat and cold that these things produce in us. But in any event there are many examples of variations in what we experience without corresponding variations in the temperature of the objects that will help convince anyone with doubts.

There is a particularly striking example which has been used by philosophers since the seventeenth century. The experiment begins by assembling three bowls of water. In one bowl the water is hot; in another bowl the water is cold; and the bowl in the middle is filled with lukewarm water. The right hand is put into the bowl of hot water and the left hand into the bowl of cold water. After a couple of minutes, both hands are transferred to the bowl of lukewarm water. The lukewarm water feels cold to the hand that has just come out of the hot water and hot to the hand that has just come out of the cold water. But the cold felt with the right hand and the heat felt with the left hand cannot both be real properties of the water in the bowl. The heat and cold experienced are only sensations produced in the observer. This is not to deny, of course, that things in the world have an objective property called temperature which can be measured by thermometers. It is merely to distinguish between the sensations of heat and cold that we feel and the temperature of the object. Generally, the higher the temperature, the hotter the sensation, but the distinction between the sensation experienced and the temperature is betrayed by cases like the experiment just described in which the same water produces different sensations by different routes. There is a significant difference between the chains of causes and effects responsible for the two sensations, since the hot hand coming from the hot water is in a very different condition from the cold hand coming from the cold water. We are aware of the hot hand losing heat and the cold hand gaining heat from the lukewarm water.

If we think of the sense of temperature as a way of determining the objective temperature of the things in our environment, we have to recognize, indeed, that this sense is subject to a quite systematic illusion. The sensations of heat and cold that we experience are directly correlated with the rate of heat loss to or heat gain from the environment, not with the real temperature of the object in contact with the skin. This means that objects somewhat below the temperature of the body will feel cool if they are good conductors of heat like metal, and warm if they are poor conductors like cork. In the same way, when the object is above the temperature of the body, it feels much hotter if it is a good conductor of heat than it does if it is not. Splashing water in a hot sauna may actually decrease the temperature of the room, but it makes it feel much hotter because the increased moisture content of the atmosphere results in a more rapid transfer of the heat to the body.

The adaptation of our sense of temperature to monitor the rate of heat gain and loss has an obvious biological appropriateness. The fact that this sense is not designed to reveal directly the objective temperature of external objects may upset the naive realist who wants to have direct cognitive access to the properties of external things. But the actual functioning of the sense is more useful in protecting the organism from damage in a hostile environment.

THE SENSE OF TOUCH

The sense of taste and the sense of temperature both conform very natural-ly to the model that I originally developed in connection with hearing and sight. But there is another fundamental sense that is much more resistant to this type of analysis—the sense of touch. In the case of sight it is natural to think of ourselves as directly perceiving the surfaces of external things, but it is not too difficult to come round to the view that we are directly aware of only images or sensations produced in us by light impinging on the retina. There appears to be, however, a much deeper conviction that through our sense of touch we are directly aware of the things with which we come into direct physical contact.

Our instinctive conviction may be partly due to the recognition that when we stretch out a hand to touch the wall, it is the wall that we touch and not some sensation produced by the wall. But the point at issue is whether we *directly experience* the sensation or the wall. We may be in direct contact with the wall through our sense of touch, in the sense that the skin of our fingers is in direct physical contact with the surface of the wall. But this does not mean that we directly perceive the wall itself rather than the sensations that are the objects of experience in other cases. On the contrary, there is a great deal of evidence in support of the conclusion that our sense of touch is just like all our other senses and not a special case.

When my finger is pricked by a pin, I say that I feel the pin, because I feel a sensation of pain from which I infer the pin responsible. When my finger is touched by the pin quite lightly, I still say that I feel the pin, al-though I feel no pain. I do experience, however, certain other sensations, certain tactual sensations, from which I infer the pin responsible. This sug-gestion is confirmed when we consider the close analogy between the ac-counts of the two situations given by the physiologist. In both cases, the pin stimulates the nervous system of the subject, albeit in slightly different ways.

Even in the case of touch, we find the sort of variation in what we ex-perience without a corresponding variation in the external object con-cerned, which led us in other cases to distinguish between the sensations directly experienced and the objective properties of the external thing. Physical things have various tactual properties: they are rough or smooth, soft or firm. What we experience when we touch a physical thing, however, does not depend solely on the tactual properties of the object.

For example, one obvious factor which influences the sensation we get is the amount of pressure we exert. There is not, indeed, the same sort of variation in apparent shape and size which we found in the case of sight. Since touch is a contact sense, there is no possibility of variations due to a change in our position with respect to the object. Even in the case of touch, however, there are some examples of discrepancies between apparent size and real size. For instance, a penny feels larger than it usually does if you pick it up when your fingers are numb with cold. Because of the abnormal condition of the fingers, what you experience is abnormal too, although there is nothing abnormal about the size of the penny. This suggests once again that what we directly experience is nothing but a sensation produced in us by the penny in contact with the skin.

If it is true that even the sense of touch conforms to the model which has been developed in connection with the other senses, it is difficult to resist the conclusion that this model has a completely general application, covering all the sensory modalities. It appears that the causal representative theory introduced in the chapter on visual perception applies in all cases.

SUMMARY OF CAUSAL REPRESENTATIVE THEORY

To sum up the discussion so far, I shall try to state concisely in general terms the causal representative theory of perception, which seems to provide so convincing an answer to the problem with which we began. It explains how we are able to acquire empirical knowledge about our environment on the basis of sense perception. According to this theory, we do not directly perceive the things in the physical world outside the body, such as tables, stars, dogs, and roses, which we normally say we perceive by our senses. Instead, such external objects must be inferred from inner objects directly experienced, which are effects produced in the perceiver by the external objects affecting the body. This theory accommodates in a completely natural way the scientific evidence concerning the various physical processes involved in the perceptual situation. And it uses this evidence to explain the fact that the similarities and differences in what we actually experience do not correspond precisely to similarities and differences in the external objects that we usually say we perceive. Sometimes, we directly experience different items when the external objects concerned are similar. This happens when there is a difference in the chain of causes and effects connecting the external object and the perceiver (i.e., when there is a difference in the conditions of observation). On the other hand, we sometimes directly experience similar items when the external objects involved are quite different. This occurs when different things produce similar effects in the experience of the perceiver, something which happens with particular frequency when the conditions of observation are less than ideal. For example, a small white dot in the visual field may be produced either by a distant rock or by a distant sheep.

Although the causal representative theory is closely integrated with the scientific account of what happens in perception, it is not itself a purely scientific theory. A purely scientific account of hearing a dog bark would begin with the vibration of the vocal chords and trace the generated sound wave until it reaches the ear. Then, the account would mention the vibration of the eardrum and the complicated mechanical processes that transmit the impulse to the inner ear. After that, we would get a story about the transformation of mechanical vibrations into nervous impulses that pass along the auditory nerve to the brain. At no point in this account is any reference made to what is actually experienced by the person hearing the dog. The sound that is actually heard is an effect produced in the perceiver by the sound waves striking the ear, but it is an effect that does not appear in the scientific story. The causal representative theory is a *philosophical* theory because it does introduce the sound actually heard and other similar items.

CHAPTER NINE

The Traditional Objection

The causal representative theory of perception holds that the things in the external physical world must be inferred from the effects that they produce in the perceiver. The traditional objection to this theory is that no such inferences can be rationally justified.

In Chapter Two, it was argued that the dogs and burglars that we normally say we hear are not really heard at all but must be inferred from the sounds they produce. Once it has been explained that this inference is not necessarily verbalized in any way, this is an extremely plausible argument. When I hear a barking noise, I am entitled to infer the presence of a dog— since in my past experience I have generally found that dogs were responsible for barking noises of this type. In the past, when I have heard a barking noise, I have frequently observed a dog in the vicinity, opening and shutting its mouth in a rhythm that correlated with the pattern of sounds heard. The inference from the barking noise to the dog on the basis of past experience is not, of course, foolproof. The barking noise may be produced by someone imitating a dog, or even, conceivably, by the branches of a tree rubbing together in the wind. Nevertheless, the inference from the barking noise to the dog is sufficiently well grounded in experience to be accepted as highly probable by all reasonable people.

The trouble begins when this account of what is involved in hearing a dog is extended to cover the perception of physical objects in general. We justify the inference from the barking noise to the unseen dog because we believe we have seen dogs barking in the past. But according to the causal representative theory, we do not really see dogs at all but only visual sensations produced in us by light waves reflected from the surfaces of dogs. The dogs must be inferred from the visual sensations directly experienced. But what past experience can justify *this* inference? If it were possible to maintain that dogs and other things may be directly perceived through the sense of touch, we could say that it is possible to infer the presence of a dog from certain visual sensations, because in the past we have noticed a suitable correlation between visual sensations of this type and dogs encountered through the sense of touch. But according to the general theory which has been developed, the sense of touch is in no special position. It functions in the same way as all the other senses. Through the sense of touch, we do not directly perceive external objects. Instead, we directly experience only sensations from which we have to infer the external objects which we say we can feel.

The situation now looks extremely serious. There appears to be a complete breakdown in the model on which we have been relying. It seemed legitimate to infer the presence of a dog from the auditory sensations experienced because we assumed that in past experience we had observed a correlation between such auditory sensations and their causes. From an effect, we can infer the nature of the cause that produced it if in past experience we have observed both effects of this type and the sort of causes with which they are regularly correlated. For example, from footprints in the sand we can infer the feet that produced them because in past experience we have observed both footprints and feet and feet making footprints. If there were even one sensory channel through which we had a direct access to things in the world responsible for the sensations we experience, we would have a way of determining the nature of the causes of our sensations; and from specific sensations we would be able to infer the presence of specific external objects, even when the direct access channel was not operating. But according to the general theory proposed, there is no sensory channel that provides us with a direct access to the external world. Therefore, we have never directly observed the external objects that are supposed to produce the sensations experienced, and hence we have never observed the regular correlation between causes and effects necessary to justify particular causal inferences. If we never directly experience dogs themselves, but only certain smells, sounds, and visual and tactual sensations, what reason do we have to believe that there really are dogs causing these various sensations? In general, what reason do we have to believe that there really are external physical objects causing the sensations we experience? It may be very natural to suppose that the various sounds, smells, and other sensations are produced by things in an external physical world, but do such natural beliefs have any rational justification?

THE THEORY OF BERKELEY

At the beginning of the eighteenth century, this very question was answered in the negative by Bishop George Berkeley. Berkeley was attacking the version of the causal representative theory that had been developed by John Locke in his *Essay Concerning Human Understanding*. According to Locke, in perception we directly experience only what he calls *ideas*. (Locke uses the term *idea* in a wider sense than that familiar today, covering things like sensations and images as well as ideas in the ordinary sense.) The ideas directly experienced in perception are effects produced in us by material objects in an external physical world that we do not directly experience. We determine the nature of the specific physical things involved on the basis of the specific ideas that we experience.

Berkeley challenged the claim that it was possible to infer from the ideas directly perceived to material substances that are supposed to produce them. Indeed, Berkeley denied the very existence of any such material substances. In Berkeley's system, the only things that exist are the ideas that are perceived and the minds that do the perceiving. Berkeley's slogan is: "To be is to perceive or to be perceived." Minds exist because they are things that perceive; ideas exist because they are things that are perceived. The material substances postulated by Locke and his friends neither perceive nor are they perceived, and therefore they do not exist.

In 1710 Berkeley published *The Principles of Human Knowledge,* in which he produced many ingenious arguments to disprove the existence of matter. The book was not well received so that three years later he published the *Three Dialogues between Hylas and Philonous,* in which he expounded the same unpopular doctrines in a more popular dialogue form. Since it was first put before the public, many have been tempted to reject Berkeley's theory as contrary to plain commonsense. Critics such as Dr. Samuel Johnson thought they could refute Berkeley by performing a purely physical act such as kicking a large stone. Berkeley was well aware of this response and did what he could to conciliate such critics who were indignant because they thought that in denying the existence of material substances, Berkeley was denying the existence of tables, stones, trees, and apples. Berkeley, however, admits and insists that tables exist, stones exist, trees exist, and apples exist. He can get away with this because he denies that tables, stones, trees, and apples are material substances. Instead, all these things are merely collections of ideas: an apple is a collection of ideas including apple-shaped colored patches, a certain smell, a certain taste, and so on. An apple is simply a collection of all the items directly perceived when one looks at, smells, tastes, or touches an apple. An apple is composed of all the ideas which the causal representative theory would regard as the effects produced by the material object affecting the senses.

If apples and tables are merely collections of ideas, then what happens to apples and tables when no one is perceiving them, since ideas are not the sorts of things that can exist unperceived? The table certainly exists when I am in the room because I am perceiving some of the ideas of which it is composed. But what happens to the table when I leave the room? Is it suddenly annihilated and then recreated whenever I come back in again? Berkeley is able to avoid a position so radically at variance with our beliefs about the habits of tables because he denies that the table is no longer perceived when the perceiver leaves the room. There is another Perceiver who never leaves the room—the Omnipresent Deity who sees and knows all. The ideas composing tables and trees and similar things are all perceived at all times by God. At any time, human beings perceive only limited selections of the ideas that exist in the mind of God. When the table is no longer perceived by human beings, it is still perceived by God, who sees everything, even what is hidden from human eyes.

Berkeley can also make use of the Divine Being to draw a distinction between the ideas that constitute real things and what he calls in the third *Dialogue between Hylas and Philonous* "chimeras formed by the imagination or the visions of a dream" (The Library of Liberal Arts, No. 39 [Bobbs-Merill: Indianapolis, New York, 1954], p. 82). Some of the ideas we experience are produced by our own imagination and some are not. Unlike the causal representative theory, Berkeley cannot attribute the ideas not formed by the imagination to external physical objects operating on the senses. Nevertheless, Berkeley does believe that these ideas have an external cause. The ideas are produced by God and have therefore a sort of objective reality not possessed by mere ideas of imagination.

Far from being obviously mistaken and an affront to commonsense, Berkeley's alternative hypothesis has certain advantages. If one already accepts the existence of God, Berkeley's theory has certain virtues of economy. John Locke and most traditional supporters of the causal representative theory also believed in God and believed that God had created the material substances that produced the experienced ideas. If we must have a God to create the material substances that are supposed to produce the ideas, it would surely be simpler for God to produce the ideas directly without bothering about material substances. In the second *Dialogue between Hylas and Philonous,* Berkeley remarks that it is not compatible with the Divine Wisdom to "do that by tedious roundabout methods which might have been performed in a much more easy and compendious way" (p. 57). If God can produce the ideas we experience by Himself, then material substances are quite unnecessary entities that can be eliminated without anyone noticing their disappearance.

Berkeley and Locke are both agreed that there must be an external cause for the ideas that we do not ourselves produce in imagination. They disagree about the nature of this external cause. For Locke, the cause is a system of physical objects; for Berkeley, the cause is a Divine Being who directly generates the ideas we experience. Both men are assuming that our ideas must have some cause, but what is the justification of this assumption? Perhaps there is no external cause. Perhaps nothing exists except myself and my own ideas.

SOLIPSISM

The doctrine that nothing exists except oneself and the ideas directly experienced is called *solipsism*. The solipsist believes that he is alone in the universe; indeed, that he *is* the universe. To avoid misunderstanding, what the solipsist denies is the existence of anything except his own *mind* or *consciousness* and the ideas it contains. He certainly does not admit the existence of his own body, which is in the same position as all other bodies, and he does not subscribe to the absurd theory that the universe is constituted by his body floating in empty space.

It may be absurd to suppose that only my body exists, but many people might argue that the doctrine that only my consciousness exists is almost equally counterintuitive. Unlike Berkeley who made every effort to reconcile his peculiar theory with our commonsense beliefs, the solipsist is uncompromising in his rejection of our most fundamental tenets. But although solipsism is difficult to believe, it is also difficult to refute. It cannot be refuted by pointing out that it has consequences incompatible with the fundamental beliefs that everyone else accepts, for the solipsist simply rejects those very beliefs. For example, if the solipsist is the universe, as he believes, then the death of the solipsist will mean the end of the universe. The solipsist will simply accept this conclusion without batting an eyelid. In any event, he may argue that he has no reason to suppose that he will ever cease to be. For the solipsist, the death of another is merely a certain series of experienced ideas, and not the annihilation of another creature like himself.

It is indeed true that there is a great deal that the solipsist cannot explain. He cannot explain why he enjoys the particular succession of ideas actually presented in his experience, but he would argue that no explanation is required. What the solipsist does, in essence, is to reject any inferences whatsoever from the items directly perceived to items that are not observed. He demands that the causal representative theory produce a watertight proof of the existence of the external world; and he demands that Berkeley prove the existence of God. Berkeley postulated the existence of God in order to make it possible for tables and trees to continue to exist when no longer perceived by human eyes, but this cuts no ice with the solipsist, who does not share Berkeley's anxiety to conform with our commonsense assumptions.

LOGICAL POSSIBILITY OF SOLIPSISM

If the watertight proof of the external world (or God) which is demanded is a logically valid deductive proof, then there is no way in which the solipsist can be satisfied. A characteristic of a valid deductive argument is that the conclusion of the argument cannot assert the existence of anything whose existence is not already asserted, at least implicitly, in the premises. Since the inference from the experienced ideas to the external physical things (or to God) has a conclusion asserting the existence of items quite different from the items whose existence is asserted in the premises, it follows that this inference cannot be deductively valid. It follows from this that we must concede the logical possibility that the solipsist is right. It is logically possible that nothing exists except myself and the ideas I directly experience and that my commonsense belief in the existence of other people and an external physical world is a total delusion. It is important, however, to see this in the proper perspective. Mere logical possibility does not amount to much. After all, it is logically possible that a cow has jumped over the moon. Unless solipsism has a somewhat stronger foundation than the report that the cow jumped over the moon, it is not much of a threat. To show that the existence of an external world cannot be deduced from the ideas directly experienced is merely to show that solipsism is not self-contradictory. Internal consistency is a necessary condition that a theory must satisfy to be given a hearing, but a theory that merely satisfies this condition has not even begun to prove its case.

DIRECT REALISM REVIVED

Solipsism has never been seriously defended by a body of influential thinkers. It has its importance in the history of philosophy because it is thought that to reduce a philosophical position to solipsism is to reduce it to absurdity. The traditional objection to the causal representative theory is that it can be reduced to solipsism because it cannot justify any inference from the ideas directly perceived to something else that is responsible for the ideas. Those who subscribe to this objection, however, do not usually go on to adopt the solipsist world view. Instead, they argue that if the assumptions of the causal representative theory inevitably lead to solipsism, there must be something wrong with these assumptions. The supporter of the causal representative theory gets into trouble with the assumption that we directly perceive only ideas and not external physical things. The critic rejects this assumption and falls back on some version of direct realism. This is a somewhat heroic measure, in view of the enormous difficulties involved in even the more sophisticated versions of direct realism, but one can understand the desperation of those who are anxious at all costs to avoid the lonely fate of the solipsist.

If one disallows the inferences to external physical things required by the causal representative theory, not in order to establish solipsism, but in order to reinstate direct realism and the commonsense view of the world, there is one very important point which must be borne in mind. A solipsist may be as severe as he pleases in his criticism of the inference to external things, without introducing any sort of incoherence into his own theory. He may, for instance, disallow any inferences that are not deductively valid. This extreme scepticism may be most implausible, but a determined solipsist can certainly take this line without undermining his own position. The direct realist, however, is not entitled to reject the causal representative theory merely because it is not able to *deduce* the existence of the external world from the ideas. If we take the view that only deductive inferences are good enough, and rule out all nondeductive empirical inferences, there is no advantage in assuming that we can perceive real physical objects and not just ideas. As he looks around the room, a direct realist might assume the existence of a desk, a lamp, a door, a carpet, some walls, and a few other things that he thinks he directly perceives. But if only deductive inferences are valid and legitimate, the direct realist is not entitled to assert the existence of anything outside the room and beyond the present range of the senses. This is surely no improvement on the fate of the traditional causal representative theory. Indeed, anyone who seriously supposes that the universe is constituted by the contents of this room is even sillier than the solipsist, whose position does have a certain perverse appeal.

The important point is that the direct realist who criticizes the inferences involved in the causal representative theory of perception must make sure that his criticism is not equally fatal to attempts to infer the many things in the universe that are not directly perceived, even on direct realist assumptions. The trick is to find principles of inference that are sufficiently strong to allow us to people the regions of space beyond the immediate range of the senses, but which at the same time are not so strong that they will permit the supporter of the causal representative theory to infer from mere ideas external objects that are never directly perceived. In the next chapter, we shall see whether or not this can be done. It is certainly not fair play to take a very hard line with the inferences required by the causal representative theory and then to become very permissive when evaluating the inferences to unperceived objects that must also be made by a direct realist.

CHAPTER TEN

The Reply to the Traditional Objection

In the last chapter, we saw that unless we are prepared to allow the legitimacy of nondeductive inferences from what we directly perceive to what we do not, we are condemned to solipsism, or to a fate that is even worse. If deductive arguments are the only acceptable arguments, then we cannot get beyond the immediate objects of experience and must content ourselves with the ideas in the mind (solipsism), or the small collection of assorted objects that happen to come within the range of the senses at any given time (direct realism). The special problem facing the causal representative theory is therefore not to be confused with the general problem of justifying nondeductive inferences which has exercised philosophers for many years under the heading, "The Problem of Induction." This problem of induction is a very complicated issue which I do not propose to open up at the present time, since it is not this sophisticated worry about induction that saps the faith of the general public in the causal representative theory. The traditional objection, as we have seen, is that the pattern of empirical inference assumed by the theory is unworkable unless there is at least one sensory channel giving direct access to the physical objects that are correlated with the experienced sensations. If we had direct access to the physical world through the sense of touch, we might be able to infer the dog we can touch from auditory or visual sensations, even when the animal itself is beyond our grasp. Past experience would set up a correlation between the sensations and dogs directly apprehended through the sense of touch. This would establish a causal connection between the dogs and the sensations, which would form the basis for future inferences. But if we experience only sensations, as the theory maintains, connections could be established only among sensations, and never between a sensation and its supposed external cause. Therefore, we would never be justified in making inferences from given sensations to objects that are not sensations.

STRICT PRINCIPLE OF CAUSAL INFERENCE

Let us try to state in abstract and general terms the principle of causal inference which seems to be involved: "If in past experience it has been observed that items of type A are regularly followed by items of type B, a causal connection between items of the two types may be assumed; and given an item of type A, the corresponding item of type B may be legitimately inferred."

If this is the only principle of empirical inference that can be recognized, it is crystal clear that the causal representative theory is doomed. It will not be possible to infer the existence of external objects that have never been observed. If we never observe external objects, we never observe regular correlations between external objects and sensations on which to base a causal inference. The most we can do is to predict what sensations we shall experience in the future. If type A sensations have always been followed by type B sensations, whenever I experience a type A sensation, I may infer that a type B sensation will be along in due course. But that is all.

If the direct realist is rejoicing in the apparent downfall of the causal representative theory, then his triumph is definitely premature. Certainly, the principle formulated above will not permit an inference from experienced sensations to their external causes. But this is because the principle, applied with absolute rigor, will *never* permit an inference from effects to causes. Suppose that I have been very lucky and have experienced in the past an absolutely regular correlation between lightning and thunder. One day my luck breaks down, and I hear the thunder without noticing the lightning which usually precedes it. Can I infer that the lightning has occurred unobserved? Not according to our principle! On the contrary, the incident must be interpreted as a counter-example which invalidates the general rule that thunder is caused by lightning.

The principle not merely disallows inferences from effects to causes: even inferences from causes to effects are severely restricted. The only unobserved effects which can be inferred are those scheduled to appear at some point in the future. If the usual effect of a given cause has not been observed to occur, we cannot assume that it has occurred unobserved. If I do not perceive thunder following a given flash of lightning, I cannot assume that it has occurred unperceived, perhaps masked by the sound of a heavy truck which was passing at the crucial moment. Indeed, this is another counter-instance which overturns the regular correlation on which inferences from lightning to thunder are based.

The upshot of this discussion is that the difficulties faced by the causal representative theory on this principle have nothing to do with the doctrine that sensations are the only immediate objects of experience. The difficulties spring from the structure of the principle itself. According to this principle, the extension of our knowledge beyond the items that are or have been directly perceived amounts merely to the anticipation of certain items that will be perceived in the future. There is no question of inferring items which have not been, are not, and will not be perceived. The known universe for the perceiver is strictly limited to items directly perceived in the past, present, or future.

It is obvious that a principle with these limitations will pose just as many difficulties for the direct realist. Certainly, the direct realist may claim knowledge of the nature and transformations of the external physical things which he thinks he directly perceives, instead of being limited to a knowledge of mere sensations. But if he adheres strictly to the principle that has been assumed to regulate causal inference, the only inferences that he will be entitled to make are inferences that will predict what physical things he shall experience in the future. He will not be able to introduce through causal inference unobserved physical things in the past or present. His physical world will be a very strange world—very limited in extent and full of gaps and blank spaces.

FLEXIBLE USE OF CAUSAL PRINCIPLE

At this point, it may be suggested that in my attempt to offer a precise and general formulation of the principle of empirical inference that we habitually employ, I have misrepresented our actual procedures. Certainly, if B has regularly followed A in past experience, it is reasonable to predict that an instance of B will follow the present instance of A. But if we require absolute regularity before we are prepared to make the inferential leap, we shall not get many opportunities to operate with the principle, however impeccable it may be in itself. For example, I shall no longer be able to predict even the regular succession of night and day if I have the misfortune to be locked up in a dark cell for twenty-four hours. Therefore, we soon learn to be flexible in our use of the principle. In particular, we soon learn to make a distinction between cases in which the failure to observe one member of a correlated pair does undermine the correlation and cases in which we may infer the unobserved presence of the missing item. If I fail to observe the descent of a stone I have thrown in the air because I shut my eyes when it reached the top of its path, it is surely absurd to take this as a counter-example to the general rule that what goes up must come down. It is much more sensible to assume that the stone has made its way back to earth undetected. A genuine counter-example would involve the positive observation of the stone continuing to hover indefinitely in mid-air, not simply the failure to observe the return of the stone to earth.

This suggestion obviously embodies good, practical commonsense. What it shows, however, is that in everyday life we do not really operate at all with the principle as originally formulated. The original principle is designed to govern an experience in which the experienced items come upon the scene in accordance with general rules and where there is nothing hidden from view. Relying on past regularities, it is possible to anticipate the future. The principle can be utilized in our experience to the extent to which it approximates an ideal experience of this type. There are certainly some regularities in our past experience. Usually, the light goes on when I pull the switch. The trouble is that the regularities in past experience are rarely complete. Usually, the light goes on when I pull the switch, but sometimes it does not, without any apparent difference in the antecedent situation. It is these irregularities in experience that necessitate the flexibility in our use of the original principle. But in the last analysis, to use a principle flexibly is not to use it at all. There must be some other set of considerations governing our procedures.

THE EXPLANATION OF PARTIAL REGULARITIES

It is the fact that we experience *partial* regularities which provides the clue to what underlies the system of causal inferences that we actually employ. If the pattern of the items experienced were completely chaotic and irregular, we would make no inferences and we would ask for no explanations: we would simply accept the random character of the given. At the other extreme, if the experienced items were ordered with complete regularity, an intellectually satisfying explanation would be available. We could say that the nature of each item is determined by the nature of its antecedents, so that everything follows from its antecedents in accordance with a rule. The actual situation, however, lies between these extremes. We experience *partial* regularities. We demand an explanation but cannot give the explanation we would give if the regularity were complete. The crucial insight is that we *can* give this kind of explanation if we assume that the experienced items form part of a wider system incorporating items that are not perceived. We can explain the fragmentary regularity of what is observed by assuming that what is observed is a fragment of a wider system in which the regularity is complete. At a single stroke, the demand for an explanation of the *partial* regularity in our experience requires us to accept both the existence of items that are not perceived and the principle that everything that happens follows from its antecedents in accordance with a rule.

Once we have introduced unperceived items, we can account for the fact that from time to time there may be exceptions to the regularities on which we usually rely. We now understand how it can happen that sometimes the light does not go on when we pull the switch. The antecedent situation appears to be the same as usual, as far as we can tell by direct observation, but we explain the different result by invoking a variation in some unperceived factor, such as a blown fuse. Moreover, once the system has been widened to include unobserved items, it is no longer necessary to treat the failure to observe the usual associate of a given item as an empirical refutation of the association. It may be that the associated item exists unobserved and in suitable circumstances its existence may be inferred.

With this liberalization of the principle of empirical inference, the direct realist can now escape the criticism which was fatal to his own position if he endorsed the argument against the causal representative theory in its original form. But perhaps the causal representative theory will also now get off the hook. At the end of the last chapter, we saw that the strategy for the direct realist must be to propose an acceptable set of principles of empirical inference that is sufficiently restricted to eliminate the causal representative theory without at the same time doing mortal damage to his own theory. The original formula knocked out the causal representative theory but also destroyed direct realism. The new proposal will allow the direct realist to construct a viable world, but is it still possible to eliminate the causal representative theory?

At first sight it appears that the causal representative theory is still in trouble. The problem is that this theory requires us to infer, not just unperceived items, but items of a kind that have never been perceived. It is quite in order for a direct realist to infer an unseen mosquito from an ominous high-pitched whine, because he has often seen the associated mosquito in the past. But according to the causal representative theory, we have never directly perceived the mosquito responsible for the whine. We still have our old problem explained in Chapter Nine. How do we infer from the whine a mosquito that has never been an ingredient in past experience, and whose association with whines has never been experienced at all, far less on a regular basis? It is one thing to use causal reasoning to fill in gaps in our experience; it is quite another thing to use it to introduce a whole new system of objects over and above the items we directly experience.

THE COMPLEX PATTERN OF CAUSAL INFERENCE

The rhetoric is impressive, but the underlying argument rests on a confusion. True enough, the only evidence on which we can base specific causal laws is a regularity that we actually experience. We find in experience items of type A regularly followed by items of type B, and we demand a causal explanation. The mistake is to suppose that the only possible explanation of the regularity is that the items of type B are caused by the items of type A. If this were the only possible explanation, causal reasoning would be limited to filling in gaps in experienced regularities. There would be no question of inferring external objects from sensations directly perceived. But in fact, there is another explanation whose possibility is implicit in the very nature of a causal system. It may be that there are other things of type X that produce the type A items, and other things of type Y that produce the type B items. The observed regular sequence may be due, not to a causal connection between type A and type B, but to a causal connection between type X and type Y. The following diagram sets out schematically this second model of causal explanation. The dotted line represents observed regularities of sequence; the arrows represent real causal connections.

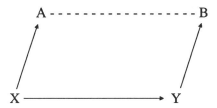

For example, the regular sequences of traffic lights are not due to causal connections among the lights themselves but to the operations of an unseen causal mechanism concealed in a mysterious box. The red light (A) is regularly followed by the green light (B), but it is not the red light that is the cause of the green light. What is responsible for the sequence of lights is a switching mechanism in the black box. In the same way, according to the causal representative theory, the regularities to be found in visual experience are not to be explained by causal connections among the visual sensations themselves. The regularities are due to causal connections among the external physical objects that produce the visual sensations.

This pattern of explanation is certainly more complex, but its complexity is a minor consideration if it provides the better explanation. The big step to take is the decision to explain the fragmentary regularities in experience by subscribing to the *principle of causality* and positing unperceived items. Once unperceived items have been introduced, there is no great virtue in economizing, if a richer system makes better sense. Whether the more elaborate system of the causal representative theory does make better sense is a question that can be decided only on empirical grounds by appealing to the evidence. The relevant evidence in support of the theory is just the traditional evidence deployed in earlier chapters. What has now been forced into the open is the theoretical underpinning for this interpretation of the evidence. Basically, the character of sensory experience has been explained as determined in part by a system of physical objects and in part by the conditions of observation. It is now clear that this system of physical objects must be posited as lying beyond experience as such, in accordance with the complex pattern of explanation for the given regularities. Without this complex pattern, we could not provide the explanation of the detail of our experience which we have given and want to give.

There is no question of reviewing all this evidence at this stage. It may be useful, however, to take a couple of fresh examples and work them through, bearing in mind the distinctions drawn in this chapter. I have chosen these examples from among the myriad available, because they seem to me particularly compelling.

TWO EXAMPLES

Let us consider, first, not the isolated visual experiences discussed until now, but the course of our visual experience as it develops over time. It is clear that our visual experience is constantly changing, and we require an explanation of the changes that take place. It is hard to see how such an explanation could be given without distinguishing between changes that are due to a change in the environment and changes that are due to a change in point of view. Operating in practice with this distinction is not usually a matter of difficulty. Quite apart from the nonvisual cues which are often available, such as the sensations associated with the acceleration of the body, there is, for instance, a distinctive pattern of change in visual experience that occurs whenever one is moving through the environment in a straight line. There is a flow pattern in which the items near the centre of the visual field gradually increase in apparent size, and those less centrally placed move gradually to the periphery before disappearing from view. (The structure of these changes is exploited by the makers of science fiction films to simulate movement through the galaxy.) We quickly learn to distinguish changes of this kind from the many changes due to real changes in the environment itself.

In everyday life, we are, of course, perfectly familiar with this distinction and have used it with success from our earliest days. My point is that this procedure, however familiar, has important implications. It definitely presupposes the complex pattern of implication I have described and introduces a domain of objects that do not appear in experience as such. The changes in my visual experience as I move through the room are not explained in terms of some law relating earlier and later members of the series of sensations that constitutes my visual experience. Ruling out a change in the room itself, the transformations in my experience are due to the change in my point of view as I move through the room. This requires me to posit an objective order to which my point of view belongs and in which it has a position. The items which belong to this objective order do not appear in the course of visual experience but are posited through the complex pattern of explanation.

Indeed, the very concept of a point of view entails the complex pattern of explanation. It is a salient feature of our visual experience, even when artificially frozen at a single moment, that it is centred about a point of view. We want to explain the content of the visual experience as a function of both the objects in the vicinity and the point of view of the experiencing subject. Thus, we introduce a system of items which lie beyond the experience of the subject, and which are posited to explain the nature of the sensations enjoyed.

My second example concerns the element of constancy in experience. The changes in experience, whose (partial) regularity is the clue that allows us to posit a world beyond experience, themselves take place, as a rule, against a background which does not change. Should we explain the lack of change in experience, when it occurs, in terms of a lack of change in the world beyond experience? Or does the content of our experience sustain itself through some kind of inertia?

There is, indeed, some tendency for visual contents to persist without the intervention of enduring external objects. The most dramatic evidence for this is the persistence of afterimages. Suppose I look at a strong source of light. When the light is put out, I continue to experience for some time a visual image which seems to have a life of its own. This case, however, is certainly the exception. Normally, the steady visual experience which I enjoy when observing a steady system of objects comes to an abrupt end when the source of light is extinguished. This suggests that the stable visual sensation experienced before depended on the steady feeding of the visual system with light waves reflected from adjacent surfaces. Thus, the constancies in experience are to be explained for the most part by reference to constancies in a domain beyond experience. The content of our experience is not as such a thing that endures: there is an appearance of endurance as the outcome of a process of continuous creation which depends on things which endure in another domain.

CHAPTER ELEVEN

The Nature of the Physical World

Even if we accept the general legitimacy of the more complex pattern of causal explanation outlined in the previous chapter, there is one final obstacle in the way of its utilization by the causal representative theory. When we use the more complex pattern in everyday life, the secret causes in terms of which we explain the regularity of the phenomena are themselves observable, at least in principle. We explain the regular sequences of traffic lights by appealing to a mechanism concealed in a mysterious box, but we can always take the lid off the box and look inside. Even when we cannot check our explanation in this very direct way, at least we can always specify the nature of the hidden causes which we take to be involved.

SPECIFYING THE NATURE OF EXTERNAL OBJECTS

The problem for the causal representative theory is that the secret causes that it introduces cannot be observed, not even in principle. How, then, can we specify the nature of the hidden causes behind the phenomena wh⁻ the only descriptive terms at our disposal get their meaning from v⁻ given in immediate experience? Unless the secret causes b⁻

resemblance to the items we experience, we cannot specify their nature. But what right do we have to assume a similarity between items in an inner world that can be observed and the counterpart items in an outer world that cannot be observed? We can never get into a position in which we can compare the inner items with the external objects in order to confirm the suggestion that they are similar.

Both direct realism and the causal representative theory admit the existence of unperceived items. The direct realist has no problem in specifying what continues to exist unperceived when he closes his eyes. What continues to exist unperceived is identical in character with the table he saw with his eyes open. The supporter of the causal representative theory may want to say that something continues to exist unperceived in order to account for the similarity of the sensations enjoyed before the eyes were closed and after they were reopened. But this something is a "something I know not what," to use the expression introduced by John Locke.

If we cannot specify the external causes of our sensations unless we assume that they bear some resemblance to the items we experience, then it is clear what we must do. We must assume that the external causes do bear some resemblance to the sensations they produce. As a matter of fact, some structural similarities are presupposed in the very formulation of the causal representative theory. The theory explains the regular succession of type A sensations and type B sensations by positing external causes of type X responsible for the type A sensations and external causes of type Y responsible for the type B sensations. This assumes that the items posited form part of the same causal system as the experienced sensations. This means that, like the experienced sensations, the external causes must also have temporal properties, bearing temporal relations to the sensations and to one another. Secondly, the external causes resemble the sensations in that they possess definite qualities and belong to definite types. It is possible, indeed, to imagine that the actual qualities of the external causes are unimaginably different from the qualities of our sensations, but even this thought assumes that the external causes are like our sensations in having definite qualities. We do not have to imagine the nature of these qualities in order to think of them as belonging to types that can then be correlated with various types of sensations. If we can posit one type of surface pigmentation producing sensations of red and another type producing sensations of yellow, we can operate the system without having to assume any similarity between the sensation experienced and the corresponding of the surface.

The point which I am making is one that must be handled with great care. It is a grave error to move from the concession that the external causes may well be *unimaginable* to the conclusion that these external causes are *inconceivable* and hence cannot be introduced into a meaningful discourse. To say that the causes are unimaginable is simply to say that they do not have qualities that resemble the qualities of anything that comes within our immediate experience, but this does not mean that we must attempt to think of these causes as things without any qualities at all. This would be a fatal move, since we cannot even conceive of a thing except as having some quality or other. But there is no reason why we should not think of a thing with a nature unlike anything we have ever experienced. Indeed, we can easily think of a whole system of such things, with a range of similarities and differences corresponding to the range of similarities and differences which we find in what we directly experience. It is a mistake to suppose that in the night all cows are black. We can certainly conceive of differentiation (as well as similarity) in a realm beyond the circle of light cast by our imagination.

DO THE CAUSES OF SENSATIONS HAVE SPATIAL ORDER?

There is, of course, the one important qualification to this doctrine that the external causes of our sensations must be conceived in a purely formal manner. The qualification is a point already made: the external causes must be represented as having temporal properties in the same sense as the sensations which come and go in our experience. Should we make a second qualification in favor of the spatial properties of things? Space and time have always been closely associated and for good reason. While they are not *things* in the universe in the ordinary sense, together they form the framework for the universe. Each appears as an unlimited extensive continuum within which limits are drawn. Thus, it would certainly be neater to have a symmetrical theory in which space and time were on a more equal footing.

I have argued that if we are to operate a system of empirical inference based on a causal principle, it is necessary to assume that the causes which we posit are organized in a temporal fashion. Is it equally necessary to assume a spatial order? The very idea of time introduces a distinction between coexistence and succession, between things that exist at the same time and things that exist at different times. Now, space is an order of coexistence. If it could be argued that we could not conceive the coexistent as a mere aggregate but only as ordered in some way, then it might follow that some general idea of space is already encapsulated in the idea of time - at least in a complex idea of time that allows for distinct but coexisting things.

THE ARGUMENT FROM IMMEDIATE EXPERIENCE

There may be something in this, but it is far too rarified an argument to rely on. I prefer to take my stand on a more concrete ground—namely, the actual nature of immediate experience. In immediate experience, we find a whole complex of simultaneous sensations—sound and smells, pains and tickles, visual sensations, tactual sensations, and so on. Moreover, these sensations are not experienced as a mere aggregate but have a certain order and structure. This differentiation of items in an order of coexistence is particularly striking in the case of the sense of sight. The content of visual experience is a visual field in which a rich complex of sensations is organized in a kind of spatial order. It may not be easy to specify the exact structure of the visual field. Certainly, it is not organized as a two-dimensional pattern, since an element of depth is clearly present. On the other hand, it is equally clear that our visual sensations are not arranged in conformity with the official three-dimensional Euclidean scheme. Nevertheless, our visual sensations do seem to have some sort of spatial properties. They appear to vary in size, in that one sensation may occupy a much larger proportion of the visual field than another. Close to an elephant, the grey visual sensation corresponding to the elephant occupies a large area in the visual field, but at the same distance from a mouse, the area taken up by the sensation corresponding to the mouse is very much smaller. Secondly, two visual sensations may be either adjacent or more distant in much the same way as two material objects may be either adjacent or more distant in physical space.

Given that the experienced sensations form this order of coexistence, it is reasonable to assume that the external causes of these sensations also form an order of coexistence, that they are arranged in some sort of spatial system. It is also necessary to make this assumption, just as it is necessary to assume that the external causes have temporal properties and belong to definite types, because otherwise it will not be possible to operate the system designed to explain the partial regularities in our experience. This system and its underlying assumptions can be justified only by its success. If we assume a spatiotemporal physical world organized as a causal system, we can make intelligible the course of our experience and can predict with some success what we shall experience in the future.

What is required by this argument, however, is merely that the physical world have some sort of spatial structure. It is not a requirement that the world be strictly subject to the laws of Euclidean geometry. If an alternative geometry proves more effective in the physical description of nature, then there is nothing in what has been said which would prevent us from assigning to this alternative geometry the special status previously reserved for the Euclidean system.

ASSUMED SIMILARITY OF PERCEIVED
AND UNPERCEIVED

In spite of all that has been said, it still remains true that the causal representative theory is assuming a certain similarity between the experienced sensations and their external causes without any possibility of eyewitness corroboration. Since we cannot inspect the external causes, we must rely on circumstantial evidence. It is worth noting, however, that direct realism faces exactly the same sort of problem. The direct realist assumes that when he closes his eyes, the visual object continues to exist unchanged in all its glory. How can he make any such assumption? How does he know that the table retains its color when it is not perceived? He cannot compare the unperceived table with the perceived table to confirm his view that they are alike in all respects. The basic problem arises inevitably for any theory that introduces unperceived items. We can describe unperceived items only if we assume that they are similar to items which we do perceive; but from the very nature of the case, there is no possibility of a direct comparison to determine whether or not the assumed similarity obtains. From this point of view, it seems, in fact, that direct realism has gone out further on the limb than the causal representative theory. The direct realist assumes an exact identity in character between the perceived object and the object that continues to exist unperceived; the causal representative theory can make do with a minimal similarity in structure.

PRIMARY AND SECONDARY QUALITIES:
JOHN LOCKE

Traditionally, supporters of the causal representative theory have argued that the external causes resemble the sensations only in certain limited respects. John Locke, for instance, made this point in the late seventeenth century by drawing his celebrated distinction between primary and secondary qualities. In "An Essay Concerning Human Understanding," Locke gives as his list of primary qualities "solidity, extension, figure, motion or rest, and number" (II.viii.9). With this list, Locke is trying to explicate the essential nature of the material things or corporeal objects that he takes to be the external causes of our sensations. By *extension* and *figure,* he means simply size and shape. By *solidity* (he sometimes uses as alternative terms *impenetrability* and *bulk*), Locke is referring to that feature of material objects in virtue of which they fill the space that they occupy. A region of empty space may have both extension and figure, but it lacks solidity. Locke maintains that the ideas of primary qualities introduced through sensation actually resemble the primary qualities themselves. (As explained before, Locke uses the word *idea* in a very wide sense to refer to any content of consciousness. The word covers sensations and images as well as ideas in the usual sense.) Our visual sensations, for instance, come in various shapes and sizes; Locke assumes similar variations in the external objects that cause the sensations. It is also reasonable to assume a similarity between certain transformations in our sensations and the motions of external objects. The idea of solidity, which Locke believes to be introduced through the sense of touch, is more problematic, but certainly, both sensations and external objects seem to share the property of *number*. (Strictly, number is a property of a certain *set* or *collection* of sensations or external objects.)

Locke calls all the other qualities that we ascribe to objects, such as colors, tastes, and smells, *secondary qualities*. These secondary qualities are nothing but the powers of these objects to produce certain sensations or ideas in the observer. There is nothing in the objects themselves that resembles the ideas of secondary qualities directly experienced. A rose is red and has a sweet scent only in the sense that it has the power, in suitable circumstances, to produce certain ideas in the experiencing subject. The red color and sweet scent that we directly experience exist only in us, and there is nothing in the rose itself that resembles the experienced color or scent.

Once this point is understood, there is a temptation to say that the rose itself really has no color and no scent. This can be misleading. Certainly, the rose itself does not have any properties that resemble the red color which we see or the sweet scent which we smell. But to say of a rose that it is red is to say that it has the secondary quality of redness; and to say that the rose has the secondary quality of redness is to say that it has the power, in suitable circumstances, to produce red ideas or sensations in our experience. Although there are some roses, such as yellow roses, that do not have this particular power, there are certainly other roses that do; and, therefore, there are certainly roses that really are red. If there were a rose that was completely colorless, it would be an invisible rose which lacked the power to produce any visual ideas whatsoever.

According to Locke, the powers that constitute the secondary qualities of an object depend on the nature of its primary qualities. A thing that possesses a given secondary quality is therefore a thing that possesses an appropriate set of primary qualities. This is equally true of those other properties of objects that are basically conceived as powers. For example, an object that has the property of brittleness is an object that has the power of shattering in tiny pieces in suitable circumstances, for example, when struck by a stone. This property of brittleness depends on the primary qualities of the object, on the nature of its physical constitution. Actually, there is no fundamental difference between the secondary qualities and the other powers that an object possesses. The difference is merely that the secondary qualities are powers to produce sensations in experiencing subjects, whereas the other powers are powers to affect (or be affected by) other things in other ways.

There is another respect in which we can draw no hard and fast line between the secondary qualities and the other powers which the object possesses. There are many cases where one and the same property of a physical thing produces both characteristic sensations in an observer and characteristic effects on other things. For example, a hot frying pan has both the power to melt butter and the power to produce sensations of heat in the observer. Because of the link-up between these two sorts of powers, it is possible to determine the secondary qualities of the object more precisely than can be done using the sensations alone. We can roughly assess the degree of hotness or temperature of an object through the sensations of heat that we get when we touch it. We can get a more exact measurement of the temperature of the object, however, through the use of a thermometer by noting the effect the object has on the length of a column of liquid in a glass tube. Hot objects not only have the power to produce sensations of heat; they also have the power to heat and hence expand other objects, including liquids. By measuring the degree of expansion, we can determine the temperature of the original object.

The power of the object to produce sensations of heat and cold and to affect thermometers is a power that depends on the nature of the primary qualities, like all other powers. A full understanding of the nature of hotness and coldness requires us to discover the specific primary qualities involved. In this case, the problem is not difficult. The temperature of an object depends on the "motion of the insensible parts," as Locke might say, or on the "average kinetic energy of the component molecules," to put essentially the same point in more scientific and up-to-date terminology.

To sum up, Locke divides the sensations or features of sensations that we directly experience into two categories. There are ideas of primary qualities and ideas of secondary qualities. Corresponding to these ideas are the two sorts of qualities possessed by objects - primary qualities and secondary qualities. The primary qualities resemble the ideas that correspond to them. The secondary qualities do not: they are nothing but powers to produce the appropriate ideas in the percipient subject.

Although Locke attached great importance to his distinction between primary and secondary qualities, his arguments in support of this doctrine are far from convincing. He has to show *both* that our ideas of secondary qualities do not resemble real qualities of external object*s* *and* that our ideas of primary qualities do resemble the actual qualities of physical things. He devotes most of his attention to the first part of this program and virtually takes the second part for granted. But as Berkeley pointed out soon afterwards, the arguments that Locke used to show that there are no objective properties resembling our ideas of colors, smells, tastes, and so on can also be used to make the same point about our ideas of extension, figure, and so on. One argument relies on the fact that there may be a difference in what we directly experience without any corresponding difference in the nature of the object concerned, as when we experience different sensations when we test the temperature of a bowl of lukewarm water with one hand recently exposed to very hot water and another hand just withdrawn from an icy bath. I used this argument to show that we directly experience only sensations and not the properties of external objects; Locke wants to use it to show that there is no *similarity* between the sensations of heat and cold directly experienced and real temperature properties of the water in the bowl. The problem for Locke is that there is exactly the same sort of variation in the case of the primary qualities. It is not just the apparent temperature of an object—a secondary quality—that varies with the conditions of observation; the apparent shape and size—a primary quality—can vary just as dramatically whenever we change our position. If these variations in what we directly perceive are taken as sufficient proof in the case of secondary qualities, they should also constitute sufficient proof in the case of primary qualities.

Another argument used by Locke exploits the comparison between our experience of heat and our experience of pain. Depending on its distance from the observer, a fire may produce either a sensation of heat and warmth or a sensation of pain. We do not imagine for one moment that the fire possesses a property that resembles our sensation of pain. Why, then, should we imagine that the fire possesses a property that resembles our sensation of heat (Cf.II.viii.16)? This argument is not entirely without force. It certainly should forestall any too easy assumption that there is a widespread similarity between our sensations and their external causes. But again the argument does not do the job that Locke intended; it does not establish the distinction between primary and secondary qualities. It raises doubts about the extent to which the external world resembles the sensations directly experienced. But it does not help us to draw the line between features of the content of experience that do resemble external objects and features that do not. It does not prove, for example, that there are no objective properties of things resembling the colors we experience; it does not prove that the experienced shapes do have their counterparts in reality.

CORPUSCULAR PHILOSOPHY

The most convincing defense of Locke's distinction between primary and secondary qualities emerges when we consider the real reason why Locke adopted this distinction in the first place. Locke drew the distinction because he accepted a certain account of the nature of the physical world. This was the species of atomism associated with the development of modern science—the so-called *corpuscular philosophy*. According to this philosophy, the physical world is constituted by material bodies of various shapes and sizes and occupying definite positions in physical space. These material bodies persist through time and may either maintain or alter their shape, size, and position. The other qualities that material things appear to possess, such as color, taste, and smell, are determined merely by the particular configurations and motions of the minute and insensible parts composing the grosser bodies that present themselves to our senses. Locke derived this account of the physical world from his friend, Sir Robert Boyle, who actually introduced the terms *primary* and *secondary qualities*. Sir Robert Boyle was basically a scientist, and he originally introduced the distinction to meet the requirements of a scientific theory. The distinction is therefore justified to the extent that the associated scientific theory is justified. This theory, in turn, is justified to the extent that it can provide a convincing explanation of the experienced phenomena. In its earlier years, this corpuscular philosophy had many conspicuous successes, including the explanation of temperature in terms of the motion of molecules. It was these successes that supported a distinction that could not be adequately defended by any of the other arguments that Locke advanced.

MODERN SCIENCE

Since the time of Locke and Boyle, however, there have been many changes in the picture of the physical world advocated by natural science. For example, a conception of electromagnetic radiation has developed which cannot be fitted into the corpuscular philosophy. There is also Einstein's theory of relativity and quantum theory. Even Euclidean geometry is no longer accepted as describing the structure of physical space. With these changes, Locke's theory is, of course, no longer defensible as it stands. But the evolution of scientific thought has not invalidated the spirit behind his approach. Scientists may no longer wish to describe the physical reality in terms of the exact list of primary qualities supplied by Locke, but the basic distinction between primary and secondary qualities remains alive. Like the account offered by Locke in his day, the account of the nature of the physical world offered by contemporary science must be made intelligible by being framed in terms, however abstract, that are drawn from experience and must be justified by showing that it provides the most satisfactory explanation of the actual course of our experience.

At an earlier point in this chapter, I argued that it was necessary to assume that the external causes of our sensations were items belonging to certain definite types and organized in a single spatiotemporal system. This is, as it were, a minimum condition of any scheme of explanation that hopes to do justice to our experience. More specific theories about the nature of what is out there in the physical world will be formulated in accordance with the ideas of every epoch and may be expected to alter as science develops and less adequate ideas are replaced by more adequate ideas.

Thus, the general answer to the question of how we can infer from the sensations produced in us the nature of the external world responsible for their production is that we should follow the methods and procedures of natural science. It is science that gives the answer to the extent that an answer is possible. We have no guarantee, of course, and in fact very little reason to believe, that the answers given by contemporary science are the final answers. It is perfectly possible that there will be a breakthrough which will allow us to clear up many of the mysteries which are plaguing present-day science. But even if our present understanding of the physical world is to be corrected by future advances, it is by no means totally false. How could we be so successful in predicting and controlling our environment if our scientific theories are totally false? In the same way, the science of the time of Locke and Boyle had its own successes and was not totally false. Science is not an all or nothing thing; it is a partial comprehension of the world in which we live which is, we hope, growing and developing as later thinkers build upon the discoveries of their predecessors.

THE WORLD OF COMMONSENSE
AND THE WORLD OF SCIENCE

Science comes to the aid of the causal representative theory at a crucial point; the theory returns the favor by dealing cleanly with a troublesome puzzle. The practicing scientist works away at his or her task of explanation and prediction without paying much heed to theories of knowledge and perception. As a result of his or her endeavors, he or she comes up with a picture of the world that is very different from the commonsense picture. There are, as it were, two worlds - a world of science and a world of commonsense. This idea of there being two worlds with duplicates for everything - two tables on which I am writing, two pens in my two right hands - was explained at length by Sir Arthur Eddington in the introduction to his book *The Nature of the Physical World* (Everyman's Library,

No. 922 [London: J.M. Dent & Sons Ltd., 1935], pp. 5-12). The world of commonsense is a world of apples, tables, and chairs actually possessing properties like taste, smell, and color. The world of science is very different. Even in Locke's day, the world of the scientist was a world of matter in motion, possessing only primary qualities and stripped of colors, tastes, and so on that we directly experience. Today, the world of the scientist is an even stranger place - even further removed from our commonsense conceptions. Which of these two worlds is the real world? Is it the world of commonsense, with the world of the scientist merely an imaginative construct useful for certain purposes? Or is it the world of science, with commonsense providing a naive picture of the world based on serious misconceptions? The causal representative theory comes down heavily on the side of the scientist. The commonsense idea of the world arises from a mistaken supposition that the things in the physical world possess properties like color and taste that resemble the sensations which these external objects produce in us. As soon as a distinction is drawn between our sensations and their external causes, it becomes clear that this is an unwarranted assumption. The scientific account of the world fares much better. The properties ascribed to external objects by the scientist are simply those properties required by the scientific theory that purports to explain the course of our experience.

CHAPTER TWELVE

Our Knowledge of the External World

The central thesis of the causal representative theory is that items exist that are not perceived but must be introduced in order to explain the partial regularities in the sensations directly experienced. In Chapter Ten, I showed how it was possible to use a more complex pattern of causal inference to infer the character of these external causes, even though a direct correlation between the sensations and their external causes could never, of course, be observed. In Chapter Eleven, I argued that we must postulate some degree of similarity between the sensations and their external causes because the items in the two categories are taken to belong to the same causal system, so that the character of the external world cannot be a total unknown. In the present chapter, I shall tackle one further difficulty which is even more fundamental. If we introduce a system of external causes for our sensations, how can we think about, talk about, and refer to this variety of items that are not directly perceived?

THINKING ABOUT THE EXTERNAL WORLD

It may take some time for the enormity of this problem to sink in. Just to think of a possible system of external causes seems easy enough; the hard part is to find enough evidence to infer their real existence and to describe

their character. In a sense, it is easy enough to think of a domain of unperceived items. It is easy because I can do it. The problem is to understand
how this act of thought is possible.

There is, indeed, a general problem about how thought is possible at
all; but somehow the problem seems less acute when the things we think
about, such as sensations, are present in immediate experience. When the
object of thought is given in this way, it is there for us to think about, and
only the most persistent philosopher continues to ask questions. But how
can we think about things that are not given?

THE THEORY OF DIRECT CONTACT

One of the attractions of direct realism, despite its serious and notorious
difficulties, is that it seems able to avoid this problem facing the causal
representative theory by maintaining that the physical objects we think
about *are* given in experience. We can think about things in the physical
world because we are in contact with these things. It is hard to reconcile
the dogmatic claim to be in direct contact with the external world with all
the evidence of an indirect causal chain connecting the state of the external object and the experience of the subject. There is, indeed, no absolute
contradiction if a distinction is drawn between the *cognitive* relation, connecting mind with its object, and the *causal* relation, connecting an event
with its effect. The direct realist may claim that a *direct* cognitive relation
is grounded in an *indirect* causal relation: the idea is that there is no need
to infer external objects as the causes of the sensations produced in us, because being affected by things in this way constitutes an immediate
knowledge of these causes.

To affirm flatly and without explanation that direct cognitive contact
between experience and its object is compatible with an indirect causal
relation appears very dogmatic; on the other hand, this "solution" is very
tempting, given our desperation to find some answer to the conundrum.
But dogmatism is not the only problem with the direct realist solution. If
we associate the cognitive relation to the object with the causal relation to
the antecedent, how come we single out certain elements among the antecedents and call them objects of perceptual experience, while ignoring
others? When I look at a table, the table is the object of my experience. It
is the table to which I acquire a cognitive relation in virtue of this use of
my senses. But there are many things that can be said to be *causes* of my

visual experience. There is the state of the cells in my retina; there is the packet of light waves entering the eye; there is the surface of the table involved; there is the source of the light which falls on the table. All these things make a causal contribution to my visual experience: what is so special about the table (or its surface) that leads us to give it the special title of perceptual object?

The direct realist may try to deal with this difficulty by simply stipulating certain criteria determining which antecedent causes count as perceptual objects and which do not. These criteria, however, would be quite complicated and would have an arbitrary and *ad hoc* character. For example, the moon is a perceptual object when its light falls on the surface of the mirror before my eyes, whereas the sun is not a perceptual object when its light falls upon the surface of the table to which my eyes are directed. It is quite a challenge to devise criteria that will put the moon example on one side of the divide and the sun example on the other.

There is, moreover, another difficulty to be faced. Just as there are causes of our perceptual experience that are not things we think about and refer to, so on the other hand, there are things we think about and refer to that are not causes of our perceptual experience. For example, we often think about things that will come to pass in the future. It is necessary to predict the future in order to make decisions about what to do. The appropriateness of my plans depends on what developments will take place in my environment. In order to act intelligently, it will be necessary to predict these developments. I will not leave the steak for my supper on a plate in the kitchen if I can predict that the dog will have access to the room.

The direct realist will have, of course, no wish to deny these obvious points. His idea is this: since the things we think about that do not causally affect our sensory experiences belong to the same system of space and time as the things that do, our direct access to the system at one point will allow us to represent the rest of the system through a kind of extrapolation. We must rely on inference, of course, to determine the specific nature of these regions of space and time to which we have no direct access and which we construct, in schematic form, by extrapolation from those regions that we apprehend directly. No explanation, indeed, is offered for this imaginative extrapolation beyond the small area of space-time illuminated by our direct consciousness, but even without this explanation, it is understandable why many people might consider this a likely story. Until some account is offered for the imaginative construction of space and time beyond the portion supposed to be directly accessible, this is, indeed, a story with a significant gap. It is important to close the gap, to the extent that this is possible. My argument will be, however, that once we understand how the gap is to be closed, the urge to assume a direct access to at least some portion of the external world will no longer seem so pressing.

IMAGINATION

I shall call the procedure by which we construct the world of space and time an act of *imagination,* following the definition of imagination given by Immanuel Kant in the *Critique of Pure Reason*: "Imagination is the faculty of representing in intuition an object that is *not itself present*" (trans. N.K. Smith [London: Macmillan, 1929] B 151). Kant uses the term *intuition* as a technical term indicating a cognitive relation to particular things. In his detailed discussion near the beginning of the *Critique of Pure Reason,* Kant explains *intuition* as the mode of knowledge through which we are in immediate relation to given objects. This intuition is possible in so far as we are affected by the given objects (the effect produced in us being *sensation*) (A 19-20 B 33-34). This looks very like the direct realist theory explained earlier, where an immediate cognitive relation is grounded on a mediate causal relation. In this passage, Kant appears to have in mind only one of the two kinds of intuition that he distinguishes - the intuition of external objects, which he calls "outer sense." To complete the account we must recognize that Kant also posits an inner sense "by means of which the mind intuits itself or its inner state" (trans. N.K. Smith [London: Macmillan, 1929] A 22 B 37). It is through inner sense that we are directly aware of our own sensations, for instance. In spite of differences between the two cases - the positing of an awareness of sensations does not require the same sort of special pleading as a belief in direct access to the external world - inner and outer sense, for Kant, are basically similar in that both involve an immediate awareness of given particulars.

It is with the introduction of the imagination that we enter radically new territory; for here we have a representation of particular things that are not given. The representation is intuitive, because it is a representation of particulars: we are not dealing here with general concepts, which form the class of representations that Kant contrasts with intuitions. But this kind of intuition is certainly puzzling, since the object is not present to be intuited. It is important to note that such acts of imagination are not to be understood as the mere having of mental images. There are, indeed, mental images that are sometimes (perhaps always) involved in acts of imagination; but these mental images are elements *within* experience, whereas an act of imagination introduces an object *beyond* experience. If on a dark night I imagine a psychopathic killer lurking around the corner, I may experience a more or less vivid mental image, but the mental image is not to be identified with the imagined killer. What I fear is not my own mental image, but a killer with the power to terminate all my mental images.

IMAGINATION AND THE FUTURE

This act of imagination whereby we represent objects which are not given is as undeniable as it is baffling. To throw light on the topic, I shall focus on what I believe is the primary field for the operation of the imagination - the domain of the future. Imaginative supplementation is certainly involved in our representation of present and past. The lion outside the door is represented through imagination; the murder of Caesar is represented through imagination. But for everyone, whatever his or her theory of perception, there is no way of representing what will happen in the future except through imagination in this sense.

This capacity to represent the future can hardly be denied, since it is, as I have already suggested, a condition of the possibility of rational action. To act rationally is to choose from among alternative courses of action, and no such rational choice is possible without a capacity to represent these alternative possibilities. The obvious question to ask at this point has the obvious answer. The question is: "How do we determine the detail of what will happen in the future?" The answer is: "By inference, based on past experience." But deeper down there is another question which is rarely faced: "How do we know that there will be a future at all?" The representation of the future is like having a vast canvas where we can paint in certain favored portions on the basis of past experience. We know where we get the paint, but where do we get the canvas?

The domain of the future which is presupposed by everyone is a structured manifold of particularity: it is an unlimited, one-dimensional extensive continuum, structured by the relation of before and after. We represent the immediate future, but we also represent a future that is more remote.

Now, the world of the future is not given in any obvious sense, since it does not yet exist in order to be given. How, then, are we able to assume that the future will come to pass?

KANT'S THEORY OF A PRIORI INTUITION

The most plausible theory, to my mind, is the one proposed by Immanuel Kant—that the original representation of future time, which grounds the possibility of detailed predictions, is an *a priori* intuition. The representation is an intuition because it is a representation of particulars; it is *a priori* because it is not based on experience but forms part of the original equipment of our representational system. Kant's theory, set out in the *Critique of Pure Reason,* is notoriously difficult, and I shall neither review the various reasons that Kant advances for his theory nor discuss what Kant takes to be the implications of his position. I shall merely use Kant's basic idea that an *a priori* intuition provides the framework for the future that we envisage—a framework that we fill out through inference from past experience but which is not itself given through experience.

Although Kant's theory of *a priori* intuition is at its most plausible in connection with our knowledge of the future, Kant himself proposes the theory as a quite general account of space and time. If an *a priori* intuition is required to make sense of the representation of the future, it is certainly not unreasonable to extend the notion and to suppose that the framework of time past and of space are also introduced through *a priori* intuition. Time future and time past form a seamless whole, and the analogy between time and space is so striking that it would be astonishing if the framework of the one was represented through an *a priori* intuition, whereas the framework of the other was represented in some other way.

If something like this is the truth, then the causal representative theory will rest on a firm foundation. We have an answer to the question of how we can introduce a system of external objects organized in space and time that will serve as the causes of our sensations. An *a priori* representation supplies the framework, whereas inferences from given sensations contribute the detail. Moreover, on this account, there is no need for, and no place for, the kind of immediate contact with external objects posited by the direct realist and by Kant himself. Since we do not have an immediate contact of this sort with the domain of the future, if the space of the contemporary world is represented in the same way as future time, then there will be no immediate contact with contemporary objects either.

PERCEPTION AND IMAGINATION

It is worth noting, indeed, that since we are basically active beings whose primary concern is not to contemplate the world but to change it, much of our attention is directed, not to the world of the present, nor to the world of the immediate past, but to the world of the immediate future. What interests me is not the *past* dinner roll in the breadbasket from which light has been reflected to enter my eyes, but the *future* dinner roll, that (I hope) will still be there when my stretching hand reaches its target. It is the representation of the future dinner roll that is involved in my project of action, and there is clearly no immediate contact between my mind and the dinner roll of the future. (I hope, indeed, that there will soon be an immediate contact between my *hand* and the future dinner roll, but that is another matter!)

One of the great advantages of the causal representative theory, as it has now been developed, is the way in which it allows us to integrate perception and imagination. I see a squirrel run up to a tree and hide behind it. I now see the tree and imagine the hidden squirrel. But the squirrel is imagined in precisely the same world as the world in which the tree is perceived. According to the causal representative theory, this is both possible and inevitable, since both the squirrel and the tree are actually represented through imagination in the technical sense. Neither the squirrel nor the tree is immediately present in experience. I say I perceive the tree and not the squirrel, only because the tree and not the squirrel is currently feeding me with appropriate sensations. This is an important difference, because it is this kind of feeding which is ultimately responsible for the detailed determination of the external world. But nevertheless, in the last analysis, the world of perception and the world of imagination are one and the same.

This representation in imagination of a world of space and time may be called *objective,* because it is not organized around a specific point of view, unlike the sensory experiences that we enjoy in immediacy. My immediate visual experience, for instance, depends on my point of view, because it is a function of the various stimuli affecting my senses, and the nature of these stimuli depends on my position in the world. The objective representation of the world of space and time, on the other hand, is what Thomas F. Nagel calls in the title of his book *The View from Nowhere* (New York: Oxford, 1986). Within this objective representation, my point of view has its own position, so that I can represent changes in my point of view in terms of which I can explain changes in my experience. I have said that our capacity to represent, refer to, and think about objects which are not present is "baffling." Is it any less baffling, now that I have identified an original consciousness of the future as playing a central role in the constitution of the imagination? I believe that it is. When the object is not present, the main problem is to prevent the object from collapsing into the representation. We may have a representation of the object, but is there an object distinct from the representation when there is no tie of presentation connecting the thing with the thought of it? When the object of representation is in the future, it must be distinct from its representation, for the simple reason that the object is in the future, whereas its representation is a present state of mind.

This story works well enough for things that will exist, but what about the things I represent that never come to be? I think about the stew I am going to make for supper and the cake I am going to have for dessert. I do make the stew, but never get round to making the cake. Neither the stew nor the cake exist at the time I am planning the meal, but the stew has some standing in the world because it actually gets made, and the future stew which gets made is the very stew I was thinking about. But what about the cake? How can it be understood as a thing distinct from the thought of it? It has no standing in the world: it is nothing but a figment of imagination.

Both the stew and the cake, however, are imagined as forming part of the future course of events. This future course of events will certainly be real, whatever form it may take. In both planning and prediction, we try to anticipate the future. This is difficult, and we often fail, positing things that never come to pass. But the posited cake does not simply evaporate, leaving behind nothing but its representation (like the smile on the Cheshire cat). There is a reality apart from the representation involved in the act of positing the cake, namely the reference to the real course of future events.

PROBLEM OF INTENTIONALITY

To interpret the act by which we represent the external causes of our sensations on the model of the act by which we represent the future course of events does indeed make the causal representative theory of perception more intelligible and more acceptable. There is still, however, a residual mystery. Neither act, as it seems to me, can be successfully explained in terms of the familiar categories that we use to describe what goes on in the universe — categories involving such ideas as efficient causality, position in space, and so on. There is no way, I think, in which the relation of an agent to his or her future, or of a thinker to his or her object, can be covered by these categories. To handle the representation of the future and the representation of the system of objects that cause our sensations, we require a radically different conceptual scheme.

Within the limits of this book, it is not, of course, possible to discuss this alternative conceptual scheme in any detail. The question is at the present time a central philosophical problem, usually referred to as the *problem of intentionality*. My book makes a contribution to the definition of this problem from the side of the theory of perception. But were I to make further moves in the direction of its development, I would soon be in deeper trouble than I want. This present chapter has been difficult enough, because it is attacking a most fundamental issue; so I shall leave you with this pointer to the problem of intentionality, without trying to take you even some way along the path.

CHAPTER THIRTEEN

The Cartesian Error

There is an important misunderstanding which has been the source of some unwarranted hostility to the causal representative theory. This misunderstanding is not one to be found only among enemies of the theory: it has been common enough among supporters. Indeed, the archvillain was Descartes himself, who did more than anyone else to introduce the modern problem of perception to the philosophical consciousness. It is worth devoting a chapter to the Cartesian error, since this has been a stumbling block which has prevented many philosophers from taking seriously the kind of theory developed in this book.

DESCARTES' METHOD OF DOUBT

Descartes appeals in his discussion to a procedure of which I made no use whatsoever in my own deployment of the problem. This procedure is his celebrated *method of doubt*. The method is to "withhold belief from what is not entirely certain and indubitable." Now, Descartes admits that he has been deceived by his senses in the past and that "it is the part of prudence not to place absolute confidence in that by which we have even once been deceived" ("A Discourse on Method, etc," translated by John Veitch, *Everyman's Library,* No. 570 [London, 1912], p. 80). Since our beliefs about the physical world depend upon the veracity of the senses, these beliefs are open to doubt and should not be accepted unless they can be reinstated by rational argument. The one thing that Descartes believes to withstand the rigors of his method of doubt is his consciousness of his own existence as a thinking thing. Thinking, in the wide sense in which Descartes uses the word, includes perceiving; although perceiving, in Descartes' book, is not a consciousness of external physical things but an awareness of things like light, sound, and heat—in other words, an immediate experience of what I have called sensations. Using this as a secure basis, Descartes eventually produces an argument to restore the physical world, removing the doubt originally introduced. We discover, indeed, that the world that we get back - the world of mathematics and physics— is not the same as the world which was taken away—the world of commonsense. The ulterior motive behind the whole Cartesian enterprise, perhaps, is to carry out just this particular feat of philosophical legerdemain.

DESCARTES' LEGACY TO THE CAUSAL REPRESENTATIVE THEORY

I shall not review the many criticisms to which the Cartesian position is exposed, because I wish to focus on the unfortunate legacy which Descartes has left to the causal representative theory of perception. The first part of the legacy is the thesis that the sensations immediately present in experience are known for what they are with absolute certainty; the second part of the legacy is the task of proving beyond any possibility of doubt the existence of the material universe. If the problem of perception is thought to be introduced by doubts about the veracity of the senses, then the only solution to the problem will be an argument that removes these doubts. The Cartesian model posits an infallible knowledge of the sensations immediately given in experience: the trick is to find a way to use this basis in a logically watertight demonstration of the existence of the external world. I certainly made no claim to accomplish such a feat. Not even Descartes succeeded, although he thought he did. Indeed, the task which has been set seems to me to be impossible in principle. There is no possible deductive move from our sensations to their external causes (see pp. 70-71).

NO INFALLIBLE KNOWLEDGE
OF SENSATIONS

The thesis that the sensations are known for what they are by an infallible intuition is certainly essential if we are trying to establish a material world that can withstand the method of doubt; but if we have abandoned this project as hopeless, there is no need to presuppose an absolutely infallible knowledge of sensations. I have made no such assumption and my argument in no way depends on any such assumption. Certainly, some of the reasons for making mistakes about physical objects cannot apply in the case of sensations. We may mistake one object for another because different physical objects may generate similar sensations; there is no comparable reason for confusing different sensations. Nevertheless, there may be other reasons for failing to discriminate sensations that are really different. Suppose, for instance, that I am looking at a blue wall where there is in fact a very slight and very gradual change in the shade of blue from the one side to the other. I may be completely convinced that the visual sensation I experience is uniform in color, but I may be wrong. I can be accused of error without self-contradiction; and it seems like mere dogmatism to insist that my sensation *must* be uniform, if I say, or think, that it is.

Suppose a subtle critic argues that it makes no sense to suggest that we may be mistaken about our sensations, since there is no conceivable way in which such mistakes could be detected or corrected. Without conceding that there is anything logically problematic about errors undetectable in principle, I would be prepared to argue that there may be convincing, even if not conclusive, reasons for regarding certain reports of sensation as inaccurate. Suppose that in the case of the blue wall the difference in shade was so slight that no difference could be detected by the naked eye, even when a dab of the paint used on the extreme right was applied to the extreme left-hand side. Then I would concede that the original sensation really was uniform. But suppose that the splotch of paint superimposed on the left-hand side was clearly visible. Then I would suspect, although I couldn't prove it, that the original sensation was not uniform after all. I shall give another example to undermine the assumption that the sensations given in immediate experience are known with absolute certainty. Suppose that there are some pennies lying on the surface of a table. If the number of pennies is large and they are heaped together, the only reliable method of counting will involve physical interaction — for example, putting the pennies into piles of ten. But if the number of pennies is fairly small, I can estimate this number simply by looking. Each penny on the table is represented by its counterpart in my visual sensation, so that I am able to count the pennies on the table by examining my sensation. But once the number of pennies on the table and their counterparts in experience gets large enough, I cannot be at all sure that I have got the number right by using the method of visual inspection; so I check my result, using the alternative penny-piling method. If I discover that the visual inspection method gave the wrong answer, I can only conclude that my estimate of the number of penny counterparts in immediate experience was mistaken.

Someone might argue that this example is unfair because the description of immediate experience involves the use of the quite sophisticated conceptual scheme of elementary arithmetic. My answer would be that this example differs only in degree from any example which could be given. Although this is not the place to argue the point, any description of immediate experience involves the application of a conceptual scheme with some degree of complexity.

FOUNDATIONS OF EMPIRICAL KNOWLEDGE

Thus, although the causal representative theory maintains that the sensations given in immediate experience form the foundation for justifying our beliefs about the external world, the theory does not require an infallible knowledge of these sensations. Our knowledge has foundations, but not foundations of *adamant* — the legendary substance with impenetrable hardness. The description of the immediate sensory presentation forms the evidence, but not all the evidence is above suspicion.

It may appear paradoxical that I am prepared to question the characterization of my own sensations, given that it is these sensations that form the foundation for the justification of beliefs about the physical world. But there are in fact many other similar structures where some revision of the evidential data can be permitted. For example, suppose I am monitoring some physical process by carefully observing my instrumentation. Even if my knowledge of the process is entirely based on the evidence of my instruments, when I review the readings I have obtained, I may come across an anomaly that I feel quite sure was due to a moment's inattention. I therefore adjust the list of readings that constitute my evidential data. In the same way, even if I use my sensations to justify beliefs about the external world, I may have grounds for adjusting the report of my sensations which I am initially tempted to give.

JUSTIFICATION OF THE EXTERNAL WORLD

It is important to be rid of the Cartesian legacy; but once it has been renounced, it may not be altogether clear why it is still necessary to justify the existence of the external physical world. A Cartesian, worried by the challenge of a sceptic who argues that the existence of the physical world is not completely indubitable, will see the point of a conclusive demonstration that the physical world exists, if it can be produced. But what is the point of the sort of argument I have deployed, which does not even claim to be logically watertight? If general reflection on the fallibility of the senses has undermined our complete confidence about the physical world, then the sort of causal argument I used in Chapter Ten will not restore us to a state of complete certainty.

Although the Cartesian dialectic and the causal representative theory may both have their beginnings in the existence of illusion and perceptual error, there is a radical difference in the ways in which the significance of this fact is understood. The Cartesian takes this fact as evidence that our supposed knowledge through the senses does not have the same indubitability as the rational intuition through which we know, for instance, the axioms and postulates of Euclidean geometry. The rationalist program of the Cartesian is hence to reconstruct a knowledge of physical nature that will have the same kind of certainty as logic and mathematics. The causal representative theory, as I understand it, takes a quite different tack. What we require is not a method that furnishes a logical guarantee that errors in perception will not happen again, but an explanation of how the mistakes were possible in the first place. The theory I have developed explains the mistakes by introducing sensations intervening between the perceiver and the external objects. These sensations are effects that are a function of the external objects and the conditions of observation. This hypothesis allows us to explain both in general and in detail how mistakes in perception are possible.

However plausible this account may be, if the result of this move is that we have no reason whatsoever for believing in the existence of external things, obviously we must go back to the drawing board. That is why it is so important to be able to show how from the sensations immediately given in experience, we can reach beliefs about a system of objects beyond these sensations. But there is no need for a conclusive demonstration: the reasonable probability provided by a sound causal argument is good enough.

Dismay at this result is to miss the point of the exercise. The objective was not to "answer the sceptic." This is the task which the Cartesian has set himself, introducing the method of doubt in the hope that he can show that the scientific story about physical nature can meet standards of rigor comparable to those of geometry and which our ordinary beliefs about the world cannot match. The Cartesian has failed; the causal representative theory has not failed, because it does not even try!

Incidentally, the position about physical nature adopted in the classical empiricist version of the causal representative theory is not all that different from the position that Descartes was trying to support. Scientists at the beginning of the modern period could no longer regard the so-called secondary qualities, such as experienced colors and smells, as real properties of physical objects. Both Descartes and Locke endorsed the scientific theory. Locke explained the situation in a straightforward way, saying that the experienced colors and smells were properties of our sensations (or *ideas,* as he called them), and that the external causes of these sensations possessed only the primary qualities assigned to them by physical scientists. Descartes wanted to maintain essentially the same view but complicated things with an ingenious and sophisticated argument involving the method of doubt, which did not work. The tragedy is that some critics, through confusion, have felt that in its argument to justify our belief in the external world, the simple empiricist version of the causal representative theory ought to meet the severe standards introduced in Descartes' complicated argumentation. This, patently, cannot be done.

I have conceded that there is no valid deductive argument that leads from the sensations immediately present in experience to their external causes. But exactly how good are the nondeductive arguments on which I rely? How strong is my proof of the external world? This question, however, conceals an ambiguity which is not always noticed. What is meant by "proof of the external world"? We can distinguish a strong conclusion and a weak conclusion. The strong conclusion states that there is a system of physical objects occupying space, that there is at least one human hand, that there is a planet called the Earth with lots of ice in Greenland and Antarctica, and on and on. The weak conclusion is that there is "something I know not what" existing unperceived and responsible for my sensations. It is a standard doctrine of inductive logic that the conclusion that makes the weaker claim has the higher degree of probability. In this case, I believe that the weak conclusion has a very high degree of probability indeed. It might even be possible to produce a sophisticated argument to show that the weaker of these conclusions cannot be coherently doubted, although I have not myself found any that is completely satisfying. But the conclusion that is more relevant for our ordinary purposes is the set of beliefs about the physical universe that we enjoy at present. To suggest that this set of beliefs is not beyond doubt and is subject to qualification is hardly an act of daring scepticism.

CHAPTER FOURTEEN

Sensation and Representation

EMERGING PROBLEMS

The struggle against philosophical problems may be compared with the battle against the hydra—the mythical, many-headed monster that Hercules finally subdued with some difficulty. The problem with the hydra was that it grew two heads to replace any that might be lopped off by a fortunate blow. In the same way, the solution to one philosophical problem often appears to uncover others. I have tried to answer the question: "How can we gain knowledge of an external world on the basis of perceptual experiences produced in us by physical objects affecting our senses?" In consequence of this attempt, a variety of other problems are now emerging. One of these problems was introduced at the end of Chapter Twelve—the problem of intentionality: "How is it possible to think about and refer to objects — both those that are given in immediate experience and those that are not?"

A second major problem which is raised by the discussion of perception and which I have not been facing is the problem of the relation between the various perceptual experiences that we enjoy and the physiological processes that go on in the brain and the nervous system. I have argued that the sensations produced in us, such as visual and auditory sensations, are effects produced by external forces impinging on our sensory systems (discounting those rare cases, like hallucinations, where the causation is internal). But these same external forces also produce complicated changes in the nervous system. For example, light falling on the retina produces changes in the area of the brain known as the visual cortex. What, then, is the relation between the visual sensation that I experience and the activity in my visual cortex?

THE MIND AND THE BRAIN

This is a special case of the large and general philosophical problem of the mind and the body, or the mind and the brain. The problem arises because I know from the inside about my own mind and consciousness, whereas I know from the outside about the functioning of brains and bodies. The problem is to put together what I know from the inside with what I know from the outside. It is tempting to suggest that the consciousness that we know from the inside is identical with brain processes that we know from the outside, just as the rainbow that we behold in the sky is identical with a certain collection of water droplets. This tempting identification, however, faces serious difficulties. One of these difficulties is the problem of intentionality, to which I have already alluded. It is difficult to see how intentional phenomena such as seeking a goal or representing a future domain of particularity could be captured in the language and conceptual scheme appropriate for the description of physiological processes. Another difficulty is to reconcile the experienced unity of consciousness with the manifold character of the population of neurons inhabiting the skull.

This is a major area of philosophical disputation and a vast literature is in existence. I cannot, in all honesty, pass over the topic in silence, since the question arises so inevitably from my discussion of the problem of perception. But on the other hand, I cannot attempt to come to grips with the complexities of the issue at the tail end of a book on another topic. (For further discussion, see, for instance, Richard Taylor, *Metaphysics,* 2nd ed. [Englewood Cliffs, NJ: Prentice Hall, Inc.], pp. 10 - 37.)

SENSATIONS AND SENSE-DATA

There is, however, a third question which I shall discuss in this final chapter. This concerns the nature of the sensations which have figured so prominently in my account. I have used the term *sensation* in a wide, technical sense because I wanted to insist on the analogy between sensations in the ordinary sense, such as pains, and the content of visual, auditory, and other sensory experiences. Just as there are sensations of pain sometimes produced by the impingement of external forces on the body of the sufferer, so there are visual and auditory sensations produced by the impingement of light waves and sound waves on the eyes and ears. In using this analogy, however, I did not commit myself to any special theory of what sensations are, nor did I try to explain how they are formed.

This is why I have avoided the term *sense-datum* (plural: *sense-data*) which has been widely used in recent years to refer to what I call *sensation*. Certainly, there is a sense in which sensations are data. They are data for the philosopher who introspects his experience, and they must be used to ground any philosophical justification of the belief in the external world. But the sense-datum theory has the further implication that the immediate content of perceptual consciousness constitutes the entire basis for our ordinary knowledge of the world. We must presuppose that our sensory system has a certain input that is a necessary condition of an information flow from the environment. The sense-datum theory maintains that the sensations constitute the terminal stage of this information flow, so that the sensations alone are accessible to the perceiver. The idea is that percipient subjects have access only to sensations laid before them, as on a plate, by ancillary physiological processes.

I am rejecting the thoroughgoing sense-datum theory because I want to distinguish between the data for the philosopher introspecting his experience—the sensations—and the data for the perceiving subject—the sensory input. As perceivers, we are not restricted to the data available to philosophical introspection. What I mean will become clearer when I produce the evidence for my position.

THE PRIMITIVE VISUAL SYSTEM

Curiously, the most compelling evidence has emerged quite recently through the study of certain rare and unusual cases. The experiencing of visual sensations is associated with the functioning of the visual cortex in the brain. After the First World War, it was determined by the Irish neurologist Gordon Holmes that if a part of the visual cortex was totally destroyed, there would be permanent blindness in a corresponding segment of the visual field. That is, even though the entire retina was stimulated in the usual way, the subject would enjoy visual sensations that corresponded to only part of the light falling on the eye. Although subjects whose visual cortex has been damaged deny categorically that they can see objects which fall within their blind patch, recent experiments have shown that they can nevertheless point to such objects with uncanny skill. This demonstrates an appropriate response to optical stimuli that does not depend on the experience of sensations. (For details, see Colin Blakemore, *Mechanisms of the Mind* [Cambridge University Press, 1977], pp. 63-65.)

There is, indeed, a physiological explanation which makes this feat more intelligible. Apparently, there are two distinct areas of the brain affected by optical information. The visual cortex is the area associated with visual experience in the ordinary sense, but there is another area in the more primitive lower brain connected to the eyes by its own system of nerve fibers. It is this lower brain center that controls the muscles of the eye when it is necessary to track the movement of some object which is of interest to the organism (e.g., as a source of food or danger). Another function of the lower brain may be to guide action when it is necessary to move quickly and *instinctively*. A stone is thrown at my head and I move my head out of the way; but I have no clear recollection of any visual sensation on the basis of which I made my move. This may well be a case where it is the primitive visual system that has saved my skin. Similarly, when the more sophisticated visual system is inoperative because of damage to the cortex, the primitive system may offer some guidance.

Although it is important to note the existence and function of this second, primitive, visual system, this discovery has, surprisingly, no direct bearing on the central question addressed in this book. This primitive system does not provide the direct access to external physical objects that is not available in the regular system. How could it? The primitive system involves a response to the sensory input, but not a direct contact with its source. Nor does the primitive system provide the sort of justification of our beliefs about the external world, such as is available through inference from visual sensations. Once people with normal visual systems are convinced that a certain object has been placed in front of a cortically damaged subject, they may be convinced, also, that the experimental subject has a way of detecting the object that does not employ visual sensations. But the efficacy of the primitive system, such as it is, can be demonstrated only by relying on the results of the sophisticated system involving sensations.

SENSORY CONTENT AS MENTAL IMAGE

What is established by the discovery of a sensory system that bypasses sensations is that the experienced sensations are not to be identified with the input of the perceptual system. In other words, the sensations and the data of sense are different. This paves the way for a suggestion about the nature of sensations which I myself find extraordinarily convincing. It is easy to assume that the sensations that we find given upon introspecting our experience are also the given element in the perceptual system; but now that a clear distinction has been drawn between sensation and sensory input, it is possible to suggest that what is given in introspection is actually created by the subject in response to sensory stimulation.

This revolutionary suggestion may be supported if we take up again an alternative concept introduced at the end of Chapter Five. This is the concept of a *mental image*. I may compare what I directly perceive when I look at a table with the mental image that I form when I try to imagine a table that is no longer before me. There has to be some similarity between what is present in perception and the mental image; otherwise, how could I tell that I had succeeded in producing the image of the table rather than the image of, say, the Great Pyramid of Cheops? The suggestion is that the sensory content immediately present in experience is a kind of mental image formed in response to the sensory input. True enough, this kind of mental image is not one which I form deliberately in accordance with previous specifications, but this is equally true of many images that we enjoy when dreaming or daydreaming.

This account of the content of sense experience also ties in with the biological story which treats perception as a function of an organism interacting with its environment - a function designed to help the organism survive in a hostile world. Primitive creatures which do not possess our kind of perceptual consciousness may nevertheless enjoy some form of perception which guides their behavior. Primitive organisms with photoreceptive spots on their outer surfaces may respond to the stimulus of light by the movement of their bodies. More complex organisms, however, have developed more sophisticated sensory systems that permit a response to the incoming signals, even when no physical movement is called for. This response consists in the forming of representations which map the external environment. Because signals often reach us from surrounding objects some time before we have to deal with these objects in a direct physical way, the sensory apparatus functions as a kind of early warning system. It provides a map of the environment, continually up-dated by fresh signals, which can be utilized by the organism in planning its campaigns.

SENSATIONS OF PAIN RECONSIDERED

Throughout this work, my fundamental thesis has been the crucial anal-ogy between the content of sense experience and sensations such as pains. Has this analogy now been undermined, in view of the reinterpretation of the experiential content as images and representations formed in response to the sensory input in order to map the external environment? Not if a suitable account is given of sensation in the ordinary sense! If there real-ly is an analogy between sounds and pains, and the sound immediately perceived is to be construed as a form of mental representation akin to a mental image, then it follows that pains too must be construed in a similar vein.

Although it is natural to suppose that the pains we feel are simply given, if we acknowledge that experienced sounds and smells are mental repre-sentations formed by the subject in response to sensory stimuli, we must say the same thing about pains. The pain that I feel in my big toe is a rep-resentation which I form in response to the stimuli coming in along the nerves leading from the toe. This account will explain the mistakes that are made when a pain is not located in the appropriate part of the body. It is well known that after the amputation of a leg, patients will often feel a continuing pain in the limb that is no longer there. The pain felt is a men-tal representation that is mislocated because it is produced by nervous im-pulses passing along the same nerves originally associated with a pain in the foot. After amputation, the train of impulses no longer originates in the foot: the source lies in the damaged nerves further along the nervous pathways. Thus, so-called feelings of pain are actually internal percep-tions of the state of the body. They involve mental representations which can be misrepresentations. We can make a mistake about the location of a pain in the same way as we can make a mistake about the location of a sound.

SENSORY REPRESENTATION

The idea that the content of sensory experience, which I have called *sensation*, is a purpose-guided response to sensory input is an idea that deserves further exploration which it cannot receive in this introductory book. If it can be shown that the content of experience is not merely the effect of external causes but also an imaginative construct designed to represent the environment, the traditional title of "causal representative theory of perception" becomes fully appropriate. Sensations can be said to represent the causes that have produced them, only in the limited sense in which an effect represents its cause. On the other hand, mental images formed in response to the sensory input are constructed with the express purpose of representing the environment that is the source of the sensory input. The artist constructs pictorial or graven images in order to represent his or her object; in perception, we all form *mental* images with the same representative purpose.

To investigate further this idea of sensory representation is to enter murky and difficult waters. It is, for instance, woefully inadequate to suppose that the stipulation of some sort of similarity between representation and object represented will get us very far. I am reluctant to undertake the task, however, not just because it is difficult, but also because it is not strictly relevant to my primary purpose in this book. This purpose is to show how one can build a knowledge of the external world on the basis of the sensations which are to be found by the philosopher who introspects his experience. This project requires us to treat the sensations as effects produced in the organism by external things affecting the senses. This is undoubtedly true, whatever further story it may be possible to tell about how these effects are brought into being.

ATTRACTION OF NAIVE REALISM
EXPLAINED

There is, however, one issue that is clarified by the idea that the immediate presentations in experience are representations. This concerns the appeal of naive or direct realism. Given that naive realism is mistaken, why is it so widely accepted among those who have not weighed the evidence against it? Why is it, to quote the words of the eighteenth- century Scottish philosopher David Hume in "A Treatise of Human Nature," that the "vulgar suppose their perceptions to be their only objects"? (*Everyman's Library*, No. 548 [London, 1911], p. 202). Why do most people confuse the items immediately present in experience with the objects populating the stage of the world upon which they are called to perform?

This confusion is much easier to understand if we recognize that the immediate content of experience is constructed in response to sensory stimuli in order to represent the environment. The sense of sight, for instance, is designed to produce a visual map of our surroundings, which will guide our behavior. It is much easier to understand how there might be a confusion between a representation and its intended object than it is to make sense of a mix-up between a sensation and its external cause. One can see how easy it would be to crunch the map which guides our behavior and the idea of the world in which that behavior takes place.

Because of the dominance of the human sense of sight, it is the visual map that tends to establish itself as the substitute for the world. Thus, most people identify external objects and visual representations. What they see is what is there. For the most part, the conceptual scheme of naive realism works smoothly enough. Certainly, visual aberrations, such as hallucinations, will cause occasional strains and stresses, but these can be handled by a species of what George Orwell calls *double-think*. As a matter of fact, the differences between the plain man and the philosophical sophisticate have little effect in practical terms. To illustrate, one bone of contention between the two systems concerns the status of the colors immediately experienced. In naive realism, these colors are real properties of physical things. In the causal representative theory, red things are not red in the sense that they have the red color we see literally painted on their surfaces: they are red, merely in the sense that the pigmentation of the surfaces has the power to produce red visual sensations in normal conditions in the normal observer. But however they may disagree about what is to be meant by yellow and black, the naive realist and the supporter of the causal representative theory are agreed that a small object, striped yellow and black, is definitely to be avoided.

Given that they identify the real dog with the corresponding visual presentation, ordinary people do not in fact infer the presence of the dog from the visual sensations produced by light reflected from its surface, in the way in which they infer the dog from the barking noises presented through the sense of hearing. This is why the idea that the dog is distinct from its visual representation, and hence must be inferred, comes as a bit of a shock. But shock or no shock, the causal representative theory of perception explained in this book, or something very like it, appears to be the only way to deal with the evidence. Through critical reflection on certain discrepancies, we become conscious of the need to distinguish between the sensory representation and the objective world it is designed to represent. To explain the detail of the discrepancies, it is necessary to treat the representation as an effect of the input from the physical world, with identifiable items responsible for specific discrepancies. Once the distinction is drawn between the physical object and its representation, it becomes necessary to justify beliefs about the physical world by showing how they can be inferred from the character of the sensory representation.

Index